fontspec pro   Feeling overwhe [FontSpec Pro. Organize your for. print out customizable spec sheet:

fontline   Convert a line of text into a bitmap for embedding into files. Add unusual graphic effects that become part of the document.

part 4: take a letter!

grammar expert   An on-line expert to instruct you on the ins and outs of English usage. Use it only when you've got a question. Get advice without a lecture!

postmaster   Envelope printing without a word processor. Click on the icon and get an envelope printed instantly, customized any way you like it.

viaprint   Imagine labels printed perfectly every time. Use your logo, multiple fonts—even special effects! This program makes great flyers and business cards too.

part 5: desktop accessories

winzip   This is a program no Windows computer should be without. With it you can instantly compress and decompress files and extract all or parts of a compressed file. WinZip supports multiple file formats.

smilershell   The ultimate utility for running DOS commands inside Windows. Neat and compact, yet stuffed with additional features to make your computing life easier.

winpost   Sticky notes with multiple uses. Set an alarm to pop up a reminder note. Attach notes to your documents.

d'menu   Turn your right mouse button into a customized menu. Add your favorite programs to a drop-down list that opens at the click of a button.

For every kind of computer user, there is a SYBEX book.

All computer users learn in their own way. Some need straightforward and methodical explanations. Others are just too busy for this approach. But no matter what camp you fall into, SYBEX has a book that can help you get the most out of your computer and computer software while learning at your own pace.

Beginners generally want to start at the beginning. The **ABC's** series, with its step-by-step lessons in plain language, helps you build basic skills quickly. For a more personal approach, there's the **Murphy's Laws** and **Guided Tour** series. Or you might try our **Quick & Easy** series, the friendly, full-color guide, with **Quick & Easy References**, the companion pocket references to the **Quick & Easy** series. If you learn best by doing rather than reading, find out about the **Hands-On Live!** series, our new interactive multimedia training software. For hardware novices, there's the **Your First** series.

The **Mastering and Understanding** series will tell you everything you need to know about a subject. They're perfect for intermediate and advanced computer users, yet they don't make the mistake of leaving beginners behind. Add one of our **Instant References** and you'll have more than enough help when you have a question about your computer software. You may even want to check into our **Secrets & Solutions** series.

SYBEX even offers special titles on subjects that don't neatly fit a category—like our **Pushbutton Guides**, our books about the Internet, our books about the latest computer games, and a wide range of books for Macintosh computers and software.

SYBEX books are written by authors who are expert in their subjects. In fact, many make their living as professionals, consultants or teachers in the field of computer software. And their manuscripts are thoroughly reviewed by our technical and editorial staff for accuracy and ease-of-use.

So when you want answers about computers or any popular software package, just help yourself to SYBEX.

For a complete catalog of our publications, please write:

SYBEX Inc.
2021 Challenger Drive
Alameda, CA 94501
Tel: (510) 523-8233/(800) 227-2346 Telex: 336311
Fax: (510) 523-2373

TALK TO SYBEX ONLINE.

JOIN THE SYBEX FORUM ON COMPUSERVE®

- Talk to SYBEX authors, editors and fellow forum members.

- Get tips, hints, and advice online.

- Download shareware and the source code from SYBEX books.

If you're already a CompuServe user, just enter GO SYBEX to join the SYBEX Forum. If you're not, try CompuServe free by calling 1-800-848-8199 and ask for Representative 560. You'll get one free month of basic service and a $15 credit for CompuServe extended services—a $23.95 value. Your personal ID number and password will be activated when you sign up.

Join us online today. Enter GO SYBEX on CompuServe. If you're not a CompuServe member, call Representative 560 at 1-800-848-8199

(outside U.S./Canada call 614-457-0802)

SYBEX
Shortcuts to Understanding

CompuServe®

The
Home Office
ShareWarehouse

Sharon Crawford

□ □ □ □ □

SYBEX®

San Francisco □ Paris □ Düsseldorf □ Soest

Acquisitions Editor: Joanne Cuthbertson
Developmental Editor: Sarah Wadsworth
Editor: Vivian Jaquette
Project Editor: Valerie Potter
Technical Editor: Karen Meyer
Book Designer: Lucie Živny
Production and Screen Graphics Artist: Charlotte Carter
Typesetter: Dina F Quan
Proofreader/Production Assistant: Rhonda Holmes
Cover Designer: Ingalls + Associates
Cover Illustrator: Harumi Kubo

The customized installation software for the enclosed programs (except Page-
Mate, Chartist, WinPost, and FontSpec Pro) was created using Small Install, a
product of Bardon Data Systems, 1023 Key Route Boulevard, Albany, CA 94706
(phone: 510-526-8470).

Library of Congress Card Number: 94-67529
ISBN: 0-7821-1569-1

Manufactured in the United States of America

10 9 8 7 6 5 4 3 2 1

warranty and disclaimer

Disk Warranty

SYBEX warrants the enclosed disks to be free of physical defects for a period of ninety (90) days after purchase. If you discover a defect in the disks during this warranty period, you can obtain replacement disks at no charge by sending the defective disks, postage prepaid, with proof of purchase to:

> SYBEX Inc.
> Customer Service Department
> 2021 Challenger Drive
> Alameda, CA 94501
>
> (800)227-2346
> Fax: (510)523-2373

After the 90-day period, you can obtain replacement disks by sending us the defective disks, proof of purchase, and a check or money order for $10, payable to SYBEX.

Disclaimer

SYBEX makes no warranty or representation, either express or implied, with respect to this software, its quality of performance, merchantability, or fitness for a particular purpose. In no event will SYBEX, its distributors, or dealers be liable for direct, indirect, special, incidental, or consequential damages arising out of the use or inability to use the software even if advised of the possibility of such damage.

The exclusion of implied warranties is not permitted by some states. Therefore, the above exclusion may not apply to you. This warranty provides you with specific legal rights; there may be other rights that you may have that vary from state to state.

Shareware Distribution

Shareware is a distribution method, not a type of software. The chief advantage is that it gives you, the user, a chance to try a program before you buy it.

Copyright laws apply to both shareware and commercial software, and the copyright holder retains all rights. If you try a shareware program and continue using it, you are expected to register it. Individual programs differ on details—some request registration while others require it. Some request a payment, while others don't, and some specify a maximum trial period. With registration, you get anything from the simple right to continue using the software to program updates. See the "What Is Shareware?" section of the Introduction for more information on Shareware.

Copy Protection

None of the programs on the disks is copy-protected. However, in all cases, reselling these programs without authorization is expressly forbidden.

acknowledgments

The world of shareware is a remarkable place. Anybody can write a program and declare themselves to be a shareware author. And they do!

But there are also some extremely talented people writing extremely good software and offering it as shareware. I met many of them in the process of writing this book. I particularly want to thank Barry Smiler, author of the SmilerShell, who also wrote the installation routines for the programs in this book that didn't come with their own. You can thank him for the fact that all the programs install with great simplicity and ease.

Others who were of great assistance include Robert Matter, Nick Naimo, Mark Jesiel, Greg Reinacker, Michael Westcott, Richard Beamish, Michael Dvorkin, Gary Chizhevsky, Steve Goings, Daniel S. Baker, Nico Mak, David Reinhart, Nobuya Higashiyama, and Casey Butler.

I also owe thanks to Sarah Wadsworth, who talked me into this project, and to Gary Masters, who sent me a ton of shareware to get me started. Val Potter organized the project for Sybex with her usual energy and good sense. Thanks to Vivian Jaquette, who edited the book with great care and kindness, and to technical editor Karen Meyer, who went over the manuscript with the proverbial fine-toothed comb. And thanks also to the usual suspects at Sybex: proofreader Rhonda Holmes, typesetter Dina Quan, and artist Charlotte Carter.

contents at a glance

table of contents

introduction

In the old days, you could set up a home office with a typewriter, a phone, maybe an adding machine, and a few sticks of furniture. These days, the investment is considerably more substantial. You need a computer (and maybe a modem and a CD-ROM drive), a fairly expensive printer, and a fax machine (maybe a scanner, too). What about a copy machine? A sophisticated answering machine for your phone? Considering voicemail?

It's no wonder that once you're finished acquiring the minimum of hardware, you barely have two nickels left for software. Probably some choices have already been made for you in the software area. For example, if you're doing medical transcriptions and your clients want the end result in a particular word processor's format, then nothing else will do. Likewise, if you're a graphic designer, there are certain programs (all expensive) that you *must* have.

Okay, so now you're down to *one* nickel. How can you afford the other software you need to make your operation more professional and efficient? The most cost-effective answer is definitely shareware. Of course, you know there are tens of thousands of shareware programs out in the world—some of them excellent and all of them reasonably priced. But who can afford to spend hours, or even days, picking through the dross to find the real gems? Not you, I'm sure.

This book can save you all that time.

what's in this book?

Inside the back cover of this book you'll find two $3\frac{1}{2}''$ high-density floppies with a total of seventeen programs for Windows. You'll need to have Windows 3.1 to run these programs.

After scouring the bulletin boards and then downloading and sifting through dozens and dozens of programs, I settled on these seventeen programs as the best ones for the home office warrior fighting the battles of time, budget, and resources.

The programs range from very simple utilities to complex applications that are indistinguishable from the most sophisticated programs found in retail stores. They're all fully functional—not demonstration or out-of-date versions. As a bonus, all the programs are refreshingly thrifty (in an age of multi-multi-megabyte Windows programs) in their use of your precious hard drive space.

The book is divided into five categories, each briefly described here.

part 1: getting organized

In this section you'll find workhorses that provide powerful functions to assist with your everyday operations. You'll find an excellent PIM (Personal Information Manager) to keep track of your schedule and programs to keep tabs on both the thing you have in abundance (information) and the resource you probably have too little of (time).

part 2: hold that call!

Probably the office machine you use the most is the telephone. Here are a couple of programs to help you tame that particular beast. One program makes organizing your phone list painless while the other lets you be in two places at once (so to speak) when you need to be.

part 3: getting graphic

I made an effort to squeeze in as many of these programs as possible. After all, except for the few graphic artists in our midst, most of us are not too great in the artistic department. These programs will keep that fact a secret from everybody (except maybe your tenth-grade art teacher, who'll *never* forget). You'll have the resources to make wonderful charts, manipulate graphic images, and keep perfect track of your font collection.

part 4: take a letter!

I've been waiting for the paperless office for what seems like an eternity—but it's not here yet. In this section you'll find programs that will let you zip out labels, print envelopes in a snap, and consult an on-line grammar expert when a question arises.

part 5: desktop accessories

To round out the collection, this section includes some handy little programs that every computer with Windows should have. Compress and decompress files, run DOS commands, and use computer sticky notes to keep your operations running smoothly and efficiently.

The descriptions in each chapter are intended to get you started with the program while pointing out the highlights. I certainly don't cover every single function, but all the important ones are described. Each program comes with good help files and/or documentation where you can find additional information.

how the programs install

In this book it is assumed that you know a thing or two about Windows and can make your way through installing the programs with a minimum of effort. If you need to know how to run Windows, I suggest you read another book—*Murphy's Laws of Windows* (also from SYBEX), for example.

Installation instructions vary a bit between programs, so there's not a one-size-fits-all set of instructions. Each program has its own chapter, so each program has its very own installation routine detailed there. (You'll be instructed to put the disks into drive A; of course, you'll use your B drive if that's the one that takes $3^{1}/_{2}''$ disks.) This way you can install programs one at a time and skip any that don't appeal to you (an unlikely scenario, I agree).

Before you actually install any of the programs, you'll be asked to copy a file to a temporary location on your hard disk. (It's important to copy the file to an empty directory, because later you'll delete the files in the temporary location.) Just in case you need a refresher, here's a quick summary: to create a temporary location, open the Windows File Manager, double-click on the C:\ directory icon, and then select File ➤ Create Directory from the menu bar. In the Create Directory dialog box that appears, type in SHARE (or a name of your choice) as the new directory's name. Now follow the installation steps outlined in the chapter that covers the program you've chosen.

The installation procedure will create a working directory for the program's files and move the files from the temporary SHARE directory you created to the working directory, so after installation you can delete them from SHARE. To do this, open the Windows File Manager, double-click on the directory, and then highlight the files you want to delete. Select File ➤ Delete from the menu bar. In the first dialog box that appears, click on OK to delete the files, and in the second, answer Yes to All.

To delete the SHARE directory when you no longer need it, open the Windows File Manager and double-click on C:\ and then the directory. Next, select File ➤ Delete from the menu bar. In the first dialog box, click OK to delete the directory; in the second, answer Yes to All.

■ ■ ■ ■ ■ ■ ■ ■ ■ ■ ■   **what if i have trouble?**

The usual routine in the software business is for everyone to disclaim any responsibility for anything (unless you pay for technical support). However, shareware is a different animal in many ways. If you have any difficulty getting the program to

■ install

■ run

■ perform any of its functions

get in touch with the programmer (whose name and number is given in the "Contacting the Programmer" section at the end of each chapter). These are real people who are strongly motivated to help you. I had occasion to talk to most of the parties involved while writing this book, and I must say they're a very nice, helpful bunch. They'll be happy to walk you through whatever's necessary to get the program installed and running as it's supposed to.

Please don't call SYBEX and please don't write to me. As much as I love these programs, I didn't write them and I can't provide technical support. (After all, I love Word for Windows, too, but I couldn't tell you why it crashes on your computer if it does!)

what is shareware?

"Shareware" is copyrighted software that is distributed by authors through bulletin boards, on-line services, and disk vendors. Copies are often passed among friends. Shareware is commercial software that you are allowed to try at home before you pay for it.

Shareware authors use a variety of licensing restrictions on their copyrighted works, but most authors who support their software require you to pay a "registration fee"—the purchase price of the software—if you continue to use the product after a trial period. Some authors indicate a specific trial period after which you must pay this fee; others leave the time period open and rely on you to judge when you have decided to use the program, and therefore should pay for it.

The shareware system and the continued availability of high-quality shareware products depend on your willingness to register and pay for the shareware you use. The registration fees you pay allow authors to support and continue to develop their products.

the programs in this book

All the programs in this book are shareware (except for FontLine, which is "freeware" that is in the public domain and requires no registration fee). They're not free, even though they may feel like it because they came on disks with the book. If you try out a shareware program and continue to use it, you are obligated to pay for it.

why you should register

As a software user, you benefit from the shareware system because you get to try the software and determine whether it meets your needs before you pay for it. Authors also benefit because they're able to get their products into your hands with little or no overhead costs for advertising and promotion. That's why you can find shareware products (like the ones in this book) that rival retail software products that cost several times the amount of the shareware registration fee.

Registering the programs you use helps preserve this remarkable phenomenon. After all, there aren't many places where you can go in and take a product home to try *on your honor*—no credit check, no contract—just honor. Shareware authors write these terrific programs and, in effect, cast their bread upon the waters. It's our obligation to see that some of that bread floats back to them.

P A R T..........

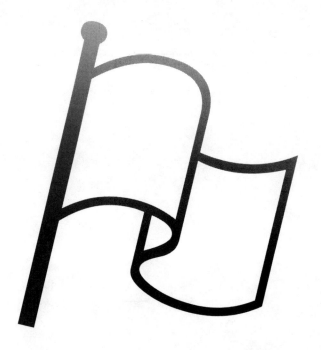

■ ■ ■ ■ ■ ■ ■ ■ ■ ■ ■

1

Getting Organized

One of the most important tasks in running your own business is keeping track of the masses of information that come your way. In this section, you'll find some excellent organizational tools for the home office or small office. They'll help you keep track of clients, schedules, and projects. If your work is complicated, these programs can help you retrieve information and juggle your schedule with just a click or two.

Program 1

Above & Beyond

Above & Beyond, billed as the PIM (Personal Information Manager) for Success, is exceptional shareware. Like all the very best programs, it has an abundance of features that nevertheless don't get in the way of usefulness. A few minutes of playing around is all it takes to get the program set up. If you want to get into the more advanced stuff later, you can. But it's certainly not required.

Above & Beyond can manage and track all of your business and personal activities. You enter recurring events such as monthly meetings just once, then enter one-time appointments as you go. You can assign priorities to different chores and let Above & Beyond dynamically configure your schedule. For keeping track of a busy life, it's an invaluable tool.

◻ **installing**

Installation is easy. Just follow these steps:

1. Put Disk 1 in drive A. Open File Manager and click on the A drive icon.

2. Highlight the file ABEYOND.EXE and then select File ➤ Copy from the File Manager menu. Copy the file to a temporary location on your hard disk.

3. Go to the directory where you've placed ABEYOND.EXE and double-click on the file name. The files inside ABEYOND.EXE will be extracted.

TIP

If the files don't show up in the File Manager window after you extract them, press F5 to refresh the view. F5 also refreshes the drive window in Norton Desktop for Windows.

4. Double-click on the file INSTALL.EXE and you'll see a window like the one shown in Figure 1.1.

5. If you *don't* want the program to have its own group inside Program Manager, click on the Add Icons to Program Manager box to remove the check mark. When that box is clear, the program will still be installed in its own directory, but you'll have to run it by double-clicking on the .EXE program from a File Manager window. This only makes sense if the program is to be used very rarely (not likely—this is a very good program!).

6. If you want the program to be in your StartUp Group, make sure that box is checked. Then click on OK.

7. If the INSTALL program finds duplicate files on your hard disk (this sometimes happens, particularly with .DLL files), it'll let you know. If the INSTALL version of the file is newer (check the date) or larger, then let it overwrite the older file.

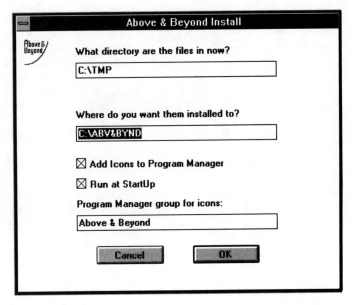

(Figure shows "Above & Beyond Install" dialog:)

What directory are the files in now?

C:\TMP

Where do you want them installed to?

C:\ABV&BYND

☒ Add Icons to Program Manager
☒ Run at StartUp

Program Manager group for icons:

Above & Beyond

[Cancel] [OK]

After installation is complete, delete all the files from the temporary location. These files aren't necessary to run the program and just take up hard disk space.

getting started

When the installation is complete, you'll have a new program group like the one shown in Figure 1.2. You can skip the Read Me file because it deals with installation, which you've already done. The Notebook is part of the Above & Beyond program (though as you can see, you can get at it here if you choose without opening Above & Beyond).

Double-click on the Above & Beyond icon to start the program. You'll be asked to supply your name. (You might as well do it—the program will keep nagging you for your name until you provide it!)

◘ **FIGURE 1.2**
The Above &
Beyond group
created by the
installation program

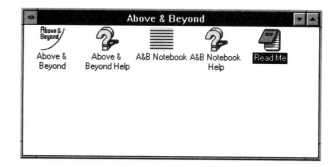

When you first open Above & Beyond, there's a whole sample schedule and files already installed. This gives you a starting point to see how Above & Beyond handles things.

TIP

Because Above & Beyond has so many features, you might want to look at the samples and try manipulating them this way and that before you start to set up your own appointments. When you get tired of fiddling around with the samples, select Delete Sample Items from the Options menu and the samples will quietly leave town.

Above & Beyond begins with three panes open, as shown in Figure 1.3. At the top is the daily schedule. The bottom left window shows the time graph, and at the bottom right is a pop-up calendar.

Click on a date on either the time graph or the calendar to open that day's schedule.

deciphering the sample schedule

At the top of the schedule, you'll see the day and date, how many items are in that day's schedule, the amount of time committed to these items, and how much time is left open. If there are conflicting items—you have more than one event scheduled for the same time period—the total overlap time is displayed. If you're looking at a previous day's schedule, the number of undone items will be reported in the banner line to make you feel guilty.

▢ FIGURE 1.3

The opening screen
for Above & Beyond

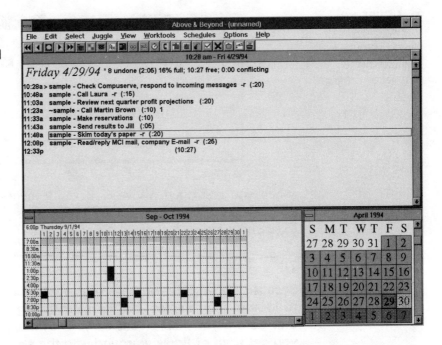

If the schedule you're looking at isn't today's, a number will appear in brackets preceded by a plus or a minus sign. If it's a plus, that's how many days the viewed schedule is in the future and, naturally, if it's a minus, that shows how many days past it is.

A greater-than sign (>) appears in front of the item scheduled for the current time, and a tilde (~) is shown before any items that have been entered as "fluid." Fluid means stuff that can be done any time within the range you specify. (There's more on fluid items in the "Workload Balancing" section later in the chapter.)

Here are the other indicators that you'll see beside items in a schedule:

-r   a recurring item

-rx   an exception to a recurring item

-a   alarm set

-ax   alarm has gone off already today

-ar   alarm has gone off already but will repeat again

At the top of the window, Above & Beyond has a toolbar with icons that are pretty easy to remember—once you know what they do. The following chart shows what each icon stands for.

◀◀	Go to previous week
◀	Go to previous day
▢	Return to today's schedule
▶	Go to next day
▶▶	Go to next week
▤	View a single day
▦	View a week at a time
▦	View a month at a time
Abc	View alphabetical list
#1	View a list by priority
◉◉	Search & find
▦	Open the calendar
⊘	Set the timer
C	Dial the phone
▤	Browse your notes
▤	Edit your notes
▦	Start the highlighted item

☑	Mark highlighted item as done
✖	Delete highlighted item
📋	Carry over undone items
🖎	Balance workload
🖨	Print a report

the time graph

The time graph (the window at the lower left) shows fixed items in red and floating items in yellow. You can set the time range under Options ➤ Settings ➤ New Item Defaults.

Double-clicking on a red or yellow item brings up the edit box for that item. Double-clicking on a blank area will open a dialog box for inserting a new item at that time and date.

The date range shown can be scrolled using the scroll bar at the bottom. To return to today's date, click anywhere in the time column. You can get rid of the time graph by deselecting it on the View menu.

the pop-up calendar

The pop-up calendar is in the lower right corner of the screen. The calendar can show any month in any year from 1987 to 2068. To change the month, use the scroll bar on the right. By default the dates with fixed items will be in light green and those with floating items will be in dark green. Days for which you have nothing scheduled are shown in gray.

Here's an easy way to move an item on the schedule from one day to another:

1. Click with the left mouse button on the item in the schedule that you want to move.

2. Click with the *right mouse button on the target date in the calendar.*

3. The item will be instantly moved to the target date. Click on the target date with the left mouse button and you'll see it for yourself!

You can remove the calendar by selecting Options ➤ Calendar ➤ Close.

creating your own schedule

When you're ready to strike out on your own, select Options ➤ Delete Sample Items and you'll be presented with a clean slate. Select the length of your workday under Options ➤ Set New Item Defaults.

TIP

One of the default settings in the Options menu is Clock Off. Deselect that item and a tiny clock will appear in the lower right corner of your screen whenever Above & Beyond is running. Click on the clock and Above & Beyond will pop open and to the front. Very handy.

adding items

To add an item to the schedule, just press the Insert key. That will cause the window shown in Figure 1.4 to open. Type in the item you want to add and specify the duration, whether it's firm or floating, scheduled or unscheduled, and so forth.

When you leave the Begin time field empty, the item is designated as "floating." This means that the item can take place in the range of time specified in Options ➤ Set New Item Defaults. Above & Beyond inserts the floating item into the schedule at the first open time, taking into account the duration of the item and other items that are already scheduled.

◘ **FIGURE 1.4**
Above & Beyond lets you enter events as memos to yourself or as specifically scheduled appointments.

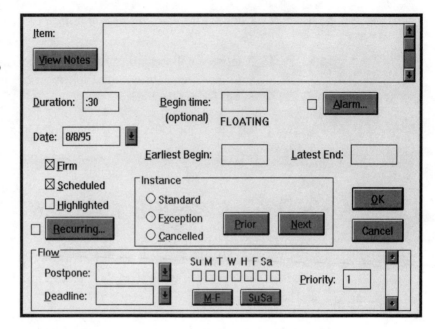

deleting items

In the daily schedule window, click on an item and press the Delete key or click on the toolbar icon with the big black X (it's shown in the chart given earlier in the chapter). You'll get a warning box and a chance to change your mind. Confirm that you want to proceed and the item will disappear.

Once you've completed an item, you can select it and click on the toolbar icon with the check mark. By default, items that are done remain on the screen, but with a line through them. A cleaner look is to have the completed items deleted from the schedule. To choose this option, select View ➤ Exclude Done Items.

workload balancing

This is one of those advanced features I mentioned at the beginning of this chapter. If you have a busy or complicated schedule, the workload balancing feature alone could make Above & Beyond indispensable to you.

Workload balancing automates the rescheduling of your undone tasks based on their priority and other factors that you determine. Any items that don't have to be tied to a particular date can be designated as "fluid" and issued a priority level. Then when you issue the Balance Workload command, all of your fluid tasks will be rescheduled automatically. Look in the Help files for specifics on workload balancing.

other features

Above & Beyond includes some very sophisticated printing options so you can define the kind of report you want to generate. You can also quickly access the Windows Notepad and Calculator from the WorkTools menu.

The commands in the Juggle menu let you move particular items to different times and days.

contacting the programmer

Above & Beyond is copyrighted 1994 by 1Soft Corporation. Comments (both positive and negative) as well as suggestions for improvement are always welcome. Registration is $149, a bit high for shareware, but A&B certainly offers value that is "above and beyond" (sorry!) the level of most shareware. Of course, registered users get unlimited technical support.

A registration form is available on the Options menu or you can register by mail, voice, or fax (they do try to make it easy):

1Soft Corporation
P.O. Box 1320
Middletown, CA 95461

Voice: 707-987-0256 (Mon.–Fri. 8 a.m.–6 p.m. Pacific time)
Fax: 707-987-3150
CompuServe: 71240,1625
Internet: 71240.1625@compuserve.com

Program 2

Account Manager

If you have to work on more than one project at once—and who doesn't?—Account Manager can automate the annoying problem of keeping track of the time spent on each one. Maybe you need to bill multiple clients or track your computer time for the Infernal…er, Internal Revenue Service. No matter what the reason, Account Manager can make the chore no trouble at all.

All you have to do is enter the projects in Account Manager and then "punch in" or "punch out" of them as appropriate. Account Manager can automatically punch in or out, or you can configure it to activate itself when an application opens or closes. At any time you select, you can create a report detailing how your time was spent.

If you don't spend all your time in Windows, Account Manager even includes a DOS interface so you can punch in or out from a DOS session.

■ **installing**

Just follow these steps to install Account Manager:

1. Put Disk 1 in drive A. Open File Manager and click on the A drive icon.

2. Highlight the file ACCTMGR.EXE and then select File ➤ Copy from the File Manager menu. Copy the file to a temporary location on your hard disk.

3. Go to the directory where you've placed ACCTMGR.EXE and double-click on the file name. The files inside ACCTMGR.EXE will be extracted.

 TIP

If the files don't show up in the File Manager window after you extract them, press F5 to refresh the view. F5 also refreshes the drive window in Norton Desktop for Windows.

4. Double-click on the file INSTALL.EXE and you'll see a window like the one shown in Figure 2.1.

5. If you *don't* want the program to have its own group inside Program Manager, click on the Add Icons to Program Manager box to remove the check mark. When that box is clear, the program will still be installed in its own directory, but you'll have to run it by double-clicking on the .EXE program from a File Manager window. This only makes sense if the program is to be used very rarely, and I think you'll be using it all the time.

6. If you want the program to be in your StartUp Group, make sure that box is checked. Then click on OK.

7. If the INSTALL program finds duplicate files on your hard disk (this sometimes happens, particularly with .DLL files), it'll let you know. If the INSTALL version of the file is newer (check the date) or larger, then let it overwrite the older file.

After installation is complete, delete all the files from the temporary location. These files aren't necessary to run the program and just take up hard disk space.

◘ FIGURE 2.1
Here's where you can specify the directory you want to install Account Manager to. You can also choose whether you want the program to be included in your StartUp group.

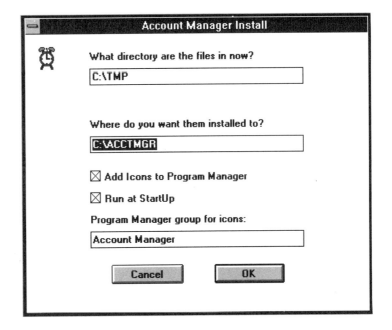

When installation is complete, you'll have a new group that looks like the one shown in Figure 2.2. Account Manager is very easy to set up the first time. Just double-click on the icon and the project list will open as shown in Figure 2.3. Enter your first project name into the list and click on the Add button (or Alt-A). Repeat until all the projects you want to track are entered.

When all the projects are entered, punch into a project by selecting it in the list and clicking on the In button (or pressing Alt-I). You can also punch in by double-clicking on the project name in the list.

getting started

■ **FIGURE 2.2**
The installed
Account Manager
group

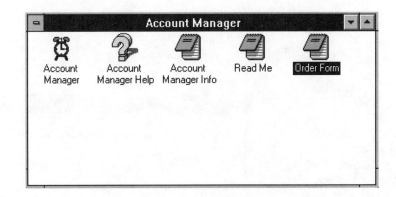

■ **FIGURE 2.3**
Starting a project list

To punch out of the project, click on the Out button or press Alt-O. Or you can punch into another project, and Account Manager will automatically punch you out of the first one.

TIP

The Prompt for Comment box means that you'll be prompted every time you punch into a project to make a note about that particular session. Remove the check if you don't need to make this note to yourself.

daily use

For regular use of Account Manager, open the program (either by double-clicking on it or by putting it in your StartUp Group) and then click on the minimize button in the upper right corner of the window to shrink the program to icon size. When no project is punched in, the icon looks like this:

To punch in, click on the icon with the right mouse button and you'll get a quick list of projects, as shown in Figure 2.4. Double-click on the project you want to start timing and Account Manager does the switch for you.

□ **FIGURE 2.4**
The project list pops open when you click the right mouse button on the iconized program.

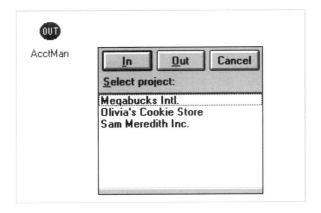

When a project is active, the icon looks like this:

The program very politely tells you not only that it's actively keeping track of your time but also just what project the time is being recorded for.

TIP

To make the Account Manager always easy to find, click on the icon once with the left mouse button. Select Icon Always on Top and the active program will always be visible.

■ ■ ■ ■ ■ ■ ■ ■ ■ ■ ■ ■ ■ ■ ■ ■ ■ ■ **getting reports**

All the information generated by your punching in and out of projects is saved into an Account Manager database. To get a report on any of that information, select Reports ➤ Create Reports and the dialog box shown in Figure 2.5 will open. You can choose from the following report types:

■ **Overall Summary by Project** shows the total time spent on each project in the list from the Starting Date shown to the Ending Date shown, inclusive.

■ **Daily Summary by Project** lists the total time spent on each project each day from the Starting Date shown to the Ending Date shown.

■ **Detailed Report** shows the time of each action (punching in or out) plus the time spent in the project for each punch in/out pair. This is the only report that displays the comments that have been entered.

■ FIGURE 2.5
Use this box to
designate the kind
of report you want.

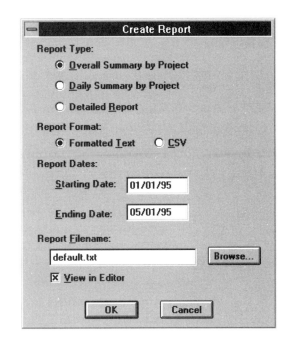

■ FIGURE 2.5
Use this box to
designate the kind
of report you want.

The report can be generated in Formatted Text or CSV, which stands for Comma Separated Values format. Formatted Text gives you a nice, clean report that you can print out if you choose. The CSV format is useful if you want to enter the saved report into a spreadsheet. Most spreadsheet programs will import a CSV file directly.

Enter a name for the report in the Report Filename box. If the View in Editor box is checked, you'll see the report in the selected editor (Windows Notepad by default). If the box is not checked, the report will still be saved under the name in Report Filename, but the editor program won't be opened.

other features

Everything in Account Manager is relevant—one of the things I like about the program is its simplicity and lack of pointless add-ons. All the features are useful and easy to use.

adjusting the database

Under the Database menu you'll find options to help you perform maintenance on your project database. You can delete certain data or correct errors. For example, let's say you're working away on a project for Garfinkle Enterprises when the doorbell rings. Off you go to chat with the Federal Express person. When you return, an embarrassingly long time later, you discover that you forgot to punch out. Well, you can correct that oversight by selecting Punch Out Earlier from the Database menu. Or if you start working and realize sometime later that you forgot to punch in, you can remedy the situation by selecting Punch In Earlier.

need more than one project list?

If you want to maintain multiple project lists, you'll find options for doing so under the File menu. Select New Project List and you'll be prompted to supply a name for the new list.You can switch back and forth between project lists by selecting File ➤ Open Project List. Click on the file name you want and then click on OK.

enabling application punch in/out

This feature is very handy if you use an application in connection with only one project. Select Application Setup from the Database menu and you can automatically punch in or out of a project when a particular application is activated, deactivated, started, or closed. For example, a particular project can be associated with Excel so that every time you activate the Excel window, that project is punched in. Multiple applications can be associated with the same project.

If you can isolate projects by application this way, you won't need to remember to punch in and out at all—except perhaps when the Fed Ex person drops by again.

when you're in dos

The DOS interface is not as slick as the one in Windows, but it works well enough to let you punch in and out when you're not in Windows at all. Open the Help files and search for DOS Interface for full instructions.

contacting the programmer

Account Manager version 1.3 is copyrighted 1993-1994 by Winnovation. Registration is a remarkably low $24.95. For that you'll get a printed manual, the latest version on disk, and unlimited free technical support. Registered users get free upgrades to versions 1.x and future updates at a good discount. Site licenses are available for multiple copies.

You can register by mail by printing out ORDERFRM.TXT and mailing it in. Credit card orders can be handled by fax.

Winnovation
P.O. Box 271071
Fort Collins, CO 80527-1071

Voice: 303-226-8682
Fax: 303-226-8682
CompuServe: 71774,605
Internet: 71774.605@compuserve.com

Program 3

Business Cards

First, I have to say that this program has nothing to do with business cards in the usual sense. It's more of a free-form database that lets you make notes on anything you choose and find the information when you need it. Unlike most programs of this type, it's easy to learn and it's very compact. The whole program plus any associated data files will fit easily on a floppy disk, so you can painlessly move it from your regular computer to a laptop and back again.

installing

Just follow these steps to install Business Cards:

1. Put Disk 1 in drive A. Open File Manager and click on the A drive icon.

2. Highlight the file BUSCARDS.EXE and then select File ➤ Copy from the File Manager menu. Copy the file to a temporary location on your hard disk.

3. Go to the directory where you've placed BUSCARDS.EXE and double-click on the file name. The files inside BUS-CARDS.EXE will be extracted.

TIP

If the files don't show up in the File Manager window after you extract them, press F5 to refresh the view. F5 also refreshes the drive window in Norton Desktop for Windows.

4. Double-click on the file INSTALL.EXE and you'll see a window like the one shown in Figure 3.1.

5. If you *don't* want the program to have its own group inside Program Manager, click on the Add Icons to Program Manager box to remove the check mark. When that box is clear, the program will still be installed in its own directory, but you'll have to run it by double-clicking on the .EXE program from a File Manager window. This only makes sense if the program is to be used very rarely.

6. If you want the program to be in your StartUp Group, make sure that box is checked. Then click on OK.

7. If the INSTALL program finds duplicate files on your hard disk (this sometimes happens, particularly with .DLL files), it'll let you know. If the INSTALL version of the file is newer (check the date) or larger, then let it overwrite the older file.

After installation is complete, delete all the files from the temporary location. These files aren't necessary to run the program and just take up hard disk space.

◻ FIGURE 3.1
Here's where you can specify the directory you want to install Business Cards to. You can also choose whether you want Business Cards to be included in your StartUp group.

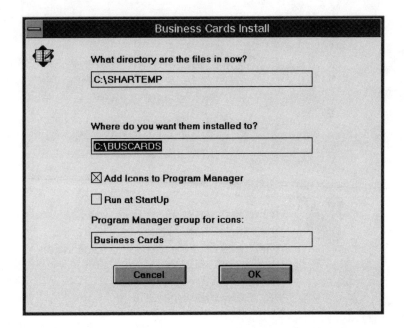

getting started

When installation is complete, you'll have a new group that looks like the one shown in Figure 3.2. Start the program by double-clicking on the Business Cards icon. After getting past the screen that reminds you to register (which doesn't appear in a registered version), you'll see the notebook shown in Figure 3.3.

Click on any one of the alphabetical tabs on the side of the book to go to that page. Type in any notes you want to make. If you keep the program iconized on your desktop, you can open it instantly whenever you need to jot down a note.

◘ FIGURE 3.2
The Business Cards group created by the installation program

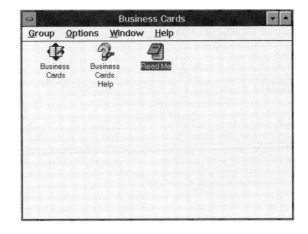

◘ FIGURE 3.3
The interface on Business Cards is one of its best features. If you can use an address book, you can use this program.

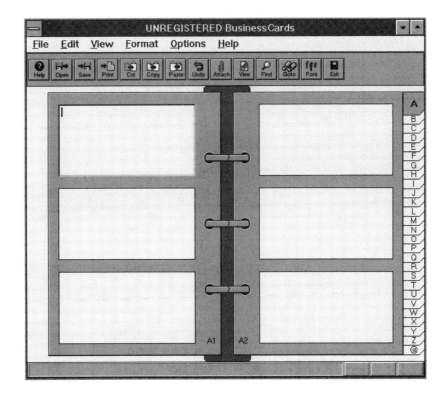

TIP
The first time you save your work, you'll have to select Save As from the File menu and enter a name for your data. If you try to select File ➤ Save, you'll get an error message instead of being prompted for a file name. Hey, it's the only flaw I found in an otherwise cool program, so I'm prepared to overlook it.

daily use

You'll probably want to configure the look of Business Cards. For example, I found the default font too small. Change it by selecting Format ➤ Font. This opens a dialog box that allows you to pick from any of the fonts on your system and designate a size as well.

To really set up Business Cards to suit yourself, you can make up your own toolbar. Select Options ➤ Toolbar. This will open up an assortment of nearly three dozen icons; some are shown in Figure 3.4. As you click on each one, its function appears at the bottom of the window, though most are pretty self-explanatory. When you find one you want on your toolbar, just click on it and then click on the icon you want to replace.

To return to the original toolbar at any time, click the Reset button.

◻ **FIGURE 3.4**
Some of the assorted icons you can put on your toolbar

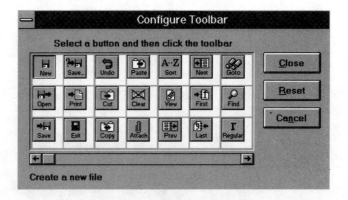

For other settings, select Options ➤ Preferences. If you get rid of the 3D effects and the exploding dialog boxes, you'll speed up the operation a bit. You can also select the number of cards on a page and whether you want them scrollable so you can fit a lot more information on each one.

searching for data

To search for a word or phrase, select Search from the View menu (or press F3, or click on the Find icon). The Search box opens as shown in Figure 3.5. Simply type in the word or words you want to find and click on the Search button. All instances of the word(s) being found will pop up in the Cards found window—along with the corresponding page number. In Figure 3.5 I'm searching for every note I've made about my business competitor, Davis.

◘ **FIGURE 3.5**
Here I've searched
for every card that
mentions Davis.

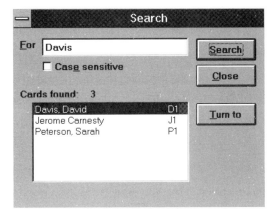

Once you have the list, you can highlight each one in turn to view it. Figure 3.6 shows a note I made about Davis while talking to Sarah Peterson.

TIP
You can type your notes on any page you want and then select File ➤ Sort. The program will put your notes in alphabetical order by the first word in the note.

□ **FIGURE 3.6**
Checking out
individual cards for
what they have on
Davis

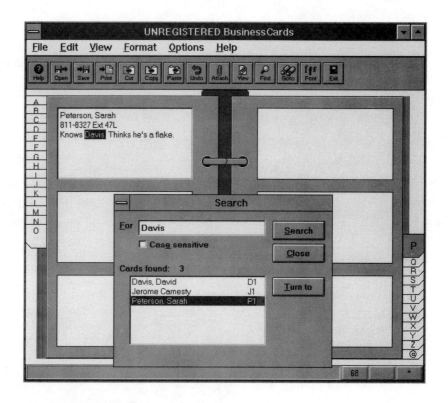

attachments

A card can have a file or an application attached to it. Select Edit
➤ Attachments. Click on the Add button and supply the information on the file you want to attach. A card with an attachment will
have a paper clip in the corner. Unfortunately, you have to move
the Attachment window aside, but it works pretty well despite that
small inconvenience. Figure 3.7 shows a card with the Windows
calculator attached.

giving cardfile the kiss-off

If you've been struggling along with Windows Cardfile, Business
Cards gives you the chance to get rid of that dorky application forever.

◘ **FIGURE 3.7**
To figure out whether Michael or Linda is offeriing me a better deal, I open the attached calculator and do some quick math.

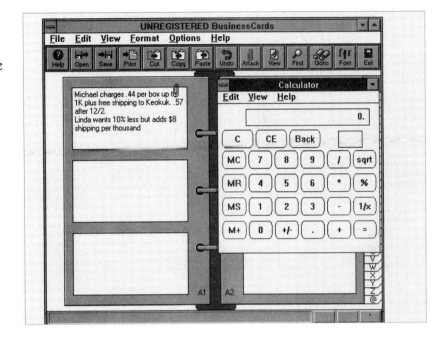

Import your Cardfile records by selecting Open from the toolbar. Select any of your saved Cardfile files (they have the extension .CRD) and then click on OK. The file will be instantly imported to Business Cards, where it can do you a lot more good.

■ ■ ■ ■ ■ ■ ■ ■ **contacting the programmer**

Business Cards version 2.0 is copyrighted 1993-1994 by Michael Dvorkin. Mike has done a terrific job with this program, especially in making it so tidy and compact. The registration fee is $19.95 and he offers a "premium" version for $24.95 with even more features. You can register in the usual variety of ways:

Michael Dvorkin
1111 Bayhill Drive #180
San Bruno, CA 94066

Voice: 415-588-6215
Fax: 415-588-6149
CompuServe: 73773,2527
America OnLine: MiD

(The opening screen also shows an Internet address, but it's no longer valid.)

Task Planner

Task Planner version 2.3 is an efficient project planner that does as good a job as the retail products do—for a fraction of the cost.

If you have to organize complicated projects in which a lot of different jobs need to be performed in the right order, Task Planner can keep you from going nuts. Instead of keeping track of a jillion little scraps of paper on your desk, just open Task Planner. When the inevitable delays occur, Task Planner can make the adjustment for you, showing how that change affects other parts of the project and what will have to be done to keep the project on track.

■ ■ ■ ■ ■ ■ ■ ■ ■ ■ ■ ■ ■ ■ ■ ■ ■ ■ **installing**

Task Planner is easy to install with the following steps:

1. Open File Manager and look in your WINDOWS\SYS-
   TEM directory for the file VBRUN300.DLL. If you see the
   file in this directory, jump ahead to step 3. If you don't
   see it, put Disk 2 in drive A and copy the file
   VBRUN3.EXE to the WINDOWS\SYSTEM directory.

2. Double-click on VBRUN3.EXE and the file
   VBRUN300.DLL will be extracted. (You can then delete
   VBRUN3.EXE to save space.)

3. Put Disk 1 in drive A if it's not there already. Open File
   Manager and click on the A drive icon.

4. Highlight the file TASKPLAN.EXE and then select File ➤
   Copy from the File Manager menu. Copy the file to a temporary location on your hard disk.

5. Go to the directory where you've placed TASKPLAN.EXE
   and double-click on the file name. The files inside TASK-
   PLAN.EXE will be extracted.

TIP

**If the files don't show up in the File Manager window after you ex-
tract them, press F5 to refresh the view. F5 also refreshes the drive
window in Norton Desktop for Windows.**

6. Double-click on the file INSTALL.EXE and you'll see a
   window like the one shown in Figure 4.1.

7. If you *don't* want the program to have its own group inside Program Manager, click on the Add Icons to Program Manager box to remove the check mark. When that
   box is clear, the program will still be installed in its own
   directory, but you'll have to run it by double-clicking on
   the .EXE program from a File Manager window. This
   only makes sense if the program is to be used very rarely.

8. If you want the program to be in your StartUp Group, make sure that box is checked. Then click on OK.

9. If the INSTALL program finds duplicate files on your hard disk (this sometimes happens, particularly with .DLL files), it'll let you know. If the INSTALL version of the file is newer (check the date) or larger, then let it overwrite the older file.

After installation is complete, delete all the files from the temporary location. These files aren't necessary to run the program and just take up hard disk space.

◘ **FIGURE 4.1**
Here's where you can specify the directory you want to install task Planner to. You can also choose whether you want the program to be included in your StartUp group.

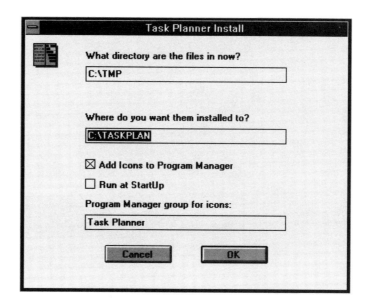

getting started

Because Task Planner is such a powerful program, it can seem a little intimidating at first. The opening screen is sort of blank and impassive, and none of the menu items appear to work! Fortunately, the program comes with a very helpful sample project. A few minutes here and you'll be zipping along on your own in no time.

Double-click on the Task Planner icon and then select File ➤ Open Project. Select SAMPLE.TSK and then click on OK. The Task Planner Work Bench will open with the sample project in place, as you can see in Figure 4.2.

◻ **FIGURE 4.2**
Task Planner comes with a sample project so you can explore the program more easily.

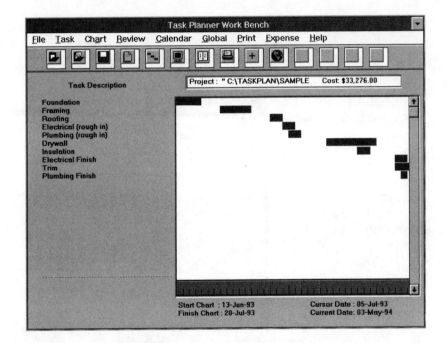

Here you see what's called a Gantt chart for a building project. Each bar in the chart represents one of the tasks in the list on the left. Move your cursor to one of the bars and a dotted line will move to the corresponding task. The Cursor Date at the bottom of the window shows the date for the point the cursor's at. All this is very interesting, of course, but how do you get the program to do something? For this you need the Task Planner tools, which are arranged across the top of the Work Bench.

the open project button

The Open Project button is the first one on the left and looks like this:

This is the button you click when you want to start a new project file. The name of the project can't have spaces or an extension and it can't be any longer than eight characters. For example, a project for the King account could be called KINGACCT. Once you've entered a name, the toolbar and the menu bar all become active.

the retrieve project button

The Retrieve Project button looks like this:

You click on this button, not surprisingly, to recall and load saved projects. You can retrieve the SAMPLE.TSK file this way or through the File menu.

the save as button

Even less surprisingly, the Save As button lets you save the project you're working on:

the task sheet

The Task Sheet is where you record all the jobs that make up a given project. The Task Sheet is reached by clicking on this button:

The information on the Task Sheet includes the following:

- ◘ The description of the individual task
- ◘ Who's responsible for the task and where they can be reached
- ◘ The start and finish dates and the cost (if any) associated with the task
- ◘ Whether or not a subsequent task depends on the completion of this one

Click on the Task Sheet button to see the Task Sheet. Highlight Foundation under Pending Task and click on the Edit button. You'll see the full sheet as shown in Figure 4.3.

Everything here is pretty straightforward. Click on any item in the Task List to see what it consists of. You can add, edit, or delete tasks. Click on OK to save your work.

The Pending Task list allows you to designate any task as critical. A critical task is one that has to be completed before another can be started.

The Pending Task area of the Task Sheet has two windows. The larger window lists all the tasks in the current project. To make any task into a critical task, scroll to it and then click on it. The task will immediately appear in the smaller window. If you decide that a particular job doesn't really have to be done before the next one starts, remove it from the smaller Pending Task window by clicking on the cl button.

◻ FIGURE 4.3
Task Sheet is ready for you to add, edit, or delete information.

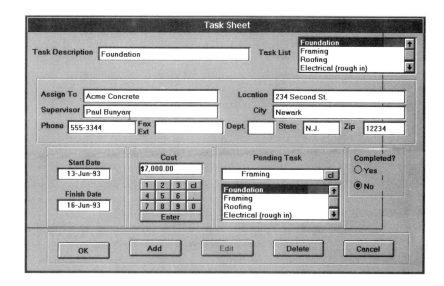

TIP
You can't designate a task as critical until you have at least two tasks entered.

the chart control button

The Chart Control button looks like this:

Task Planner displays a chart representation of the project currently running whenever you're on the Work Bench screen. The Chart Control button opens a dialog box where you can add some refinements:

◻ To zoom in on some part of the project, click on one of the date windows. A calendar will open and you can specify the period you want to look at.

◻ Check the Warning bar box, and any task not completed by its finishing date will display a bright yellow warning.

- Check the Critical bar box, and any critical (pending) task not completed on time will display a bright red bar showing that the next part of the project is being delayed.

the review button

Click on the Review button to bring up a list of all the tasks of the current project. This list will include the name of the task, the start and finish dates, and the name of the responsible person (if any). The Review button looks like this:

the calendar button

Click on the Calendar button at any point to bring up a current calendar. Buttons in the upper left corner of the window let you change the display. The Calendar button looks, as you might suspect, a bit like a calendar:

the printer button

To print out any part of your project, click on the Printer button:

You can print the chart, the task list or any part of it, as well as reports on additional expenses.

the expense button

When those inevitable additional expenses crop up, click on this button:

This opens a window where you can record the amount and a description of costs that aren't in the Task Sheet. Click on Enter after each cost and click on Add to record each item into the project.

the global button

Click on the Global button when dates have to be rescheduled. The Global button looks like this:

Set the Start Date and Finish Date to include all the tasks that have to be rescheduled—in other words, any task that *starts* between those two dates. In the # of days box, tell the program how many days you want to shift. A positive number means that all the tasks being rescheduled will be delayed by that many days. A negative number means that the starting date for these tasks will be that many days earlier.

If you set the Confirm Each Task box to Yes, rescheduled tasks will be displayed and you'll be able to confirm or pass on each one.

▫ ▫ ▫ ▫ ▫ ▫ ▫ ▫ contacting the programmer

Task Planner version 2.3 is copyrighted 1994 by InfoWare Solutions, Inc., and was written by the very clever Richard Beamish.

You can address questions to him on CompuServe: 74003,757. Registration costs $49 (U.S. dollars). Send a check or money order to:

InfoWare Solutions, Inc.
P.O. Box 7256
1355 Richmond Road
Ottawa, Ontario
Canada K2A 4E3

If you're in Canada, it'll cost you more. Send $62 in Canadian dollars plus $4.34 GST. Ontario folk are hit for an additional $4.96 in GST.

Credit card orders can be placed by calling 800-242-4775, or you can fax an order to 713-524-6398. These numbers are for the Public Software Library, which represents a lot of shareware authors. The order number for Task Planner is 11208.

P A R T . . . .

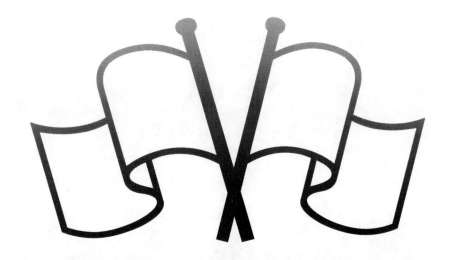

■ ■ ■ ■ ■ ■ ■ ■ ■ ■

2

Hold That Call!

When you work at home, the phone can be both your lifeline and your biggest pain in the neck. Keeping track of lots of numbers and sometimes just keeping in touch at all can be major challenges. Here are a couple of programs that can help you stay connected—and help you save some money, too.

Practical PhoneBook

Like me, you probably already have a number of programs (including the Windows Cardfile) that'll dial your phone for you if your computer has a modem and you have a telephone on the same line. But many times, I'd just like to click on an icon, select a name from a list, and have the number dialed for me. I don't want to bother with opening a big program and poking around to find the part that has the phone listings.

Practical PhoneBook is a model of simplicity and ease. Add it to your StartUp group and you can keep it minimized on your desktop, where it's just a mouse-click away.

■ ■ ■ ■ ■ ■ ■ ■ ■ ■ ■ ■ ■ ■ ■ ■ ■ ■ **installing**

Just follow these steps to install Practical PhoneBook:

1. Put Disk 1 in drive A. Open File Manager and click on the A drive icon.

2. Highlight the file PHONEBK.EXE and then select File ➤ Copy from the File Manager menu. Copy the file to a temporary location on your hard disk.

3. Go to the directory where you've placed PHONEBK.EXE and double-click on the file name. The files inside PHONEBK.EXE will be extracted.

 TIP

If the files don't show up in the File Manager window after you extract them, press F5 to refresh the view. F5 also refreshes the drive window in Norton Desktop for Windows.

4. Double-click on the file INSTALL.EXE and you'll see a window like the one shown in Figure 5.1.

5. If you *don't* want the program to have its own group inside Program Manager, click on the Add Icons to Program Manager box to remove the check mark. When that box is clear, the program will still be installed in its own directory, but you'll have to run it by double-clicking on the .EXE program from a File Manager window. This only makes sense if the program is to be used very rarely.

6. If you want the program to be in your StartUp group, make sure that box is checked. Then click on OK.

7. If the INSTALL program finds duplicate files on your hard disk (this sometimes happens, particularly with .DLL files), it'll let you know. If the INSTALL version of the file is newer (check the date) or larger, then let it overwrite the older file.

After installation is complete, delete all the files from the temporary location. These files aren't necessary to run the program and just take up hard disk space.

◻ **FIGURE 5.1**
Here's where you can specify the directory you want to install Practical PhoneBook to. You can also choose whether you want the program to be included in your StartUp group.

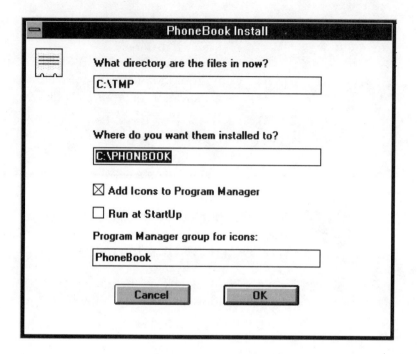

getting started

To build your own phone list, double-click on the PhoneBook icon. This'll give you a blank slate to start with. Click on the Add button and then fill in the name and phone number for each person or company you want on your phone list. Click on the Next button to move on to another entry.

In addition to the name and number, you can include lots of information about the party you'll be calling, as shown in Figure 5.2. You can distinguish between work, home, and car phone numbers. There's a selection of other possible identifiers in the drop-down list next to Other. In the Notes box, jot down any memory-joggers you might need about the person you're calling.

◘ **FIGURE 5.2**
You can limit an entry to just a name and number or you can include detailed notes.

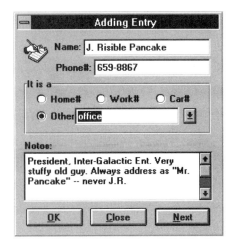

Click on OK when you've made your final entry (for now—you can always go back and add more names). Then all you have to do is double-click on any name on the list and the program will dial the number and tell you when to pick up the phone.

TIP
Practical PhoneBook is very good at scoping out your system and determining the facts about your modem—but no program is perfect. If you're not getting results when you try to dial, select Settings ➤ Dial Settings to make sure that Practical PhoneBook is looking for your modem on the right COM port.

◘ ◘ ◘ ◘ ◘ ◘ ◘ ◘ ◘ ◘ ◘ ◘ ◘ ◘ ◘ ◘ ◘ ◘ ◘ **daily use**

Once you have all your numbers entered, you can park Practical PhoneBook on your desk in a number of different formats. I like to drag the borders so it's a single column of names, and then minimize it. When I open it back up, it looks like Figure 5.3. It will stay in this format until I change it, even after the program is closed and opened again.

□ **FIGURE 5.3**
One way of displaying Practical PhoneBook. The icons to the left of some names indicate that there's a note attached to them.

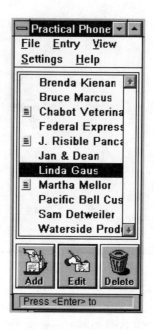

If you have a lot of phone numbers—Practical Phonebook will accommodate up to about 2,000 entries—you might want to select View ➤ Alphabet Box. When this entry is toggled on, a keyboard is available at the bottom of the PhoneBook window. Click on a letter to zip to entries beginning with that letter.

changing the look

Some options for changing the look of PhoneBook can be found by selecting Settings ➤ Display Settings. Here's what the options mean:

Show phone number type   Clear this box if you don't want the listing to include what kind of phone number this is.

Show name and phone # in columns   Check this box if you want everything in neat columns.

Show notes icon	Check this box to show which numbers have notes attached to them.
Enable horizontal scrolling	Check this box to get a scroll bar at the bottom of the window.
Show call timer	When this box is checked, a timer will appear at the bottom of the window at the beginning of a call. This is handy for keeping your phone bill down.

other features

If you have a lot of numbers in your phone list, you may want to keep the really important numbers (like the one for pizza delivery) on a Quick List. Highlight a listing and then select Entry ➤ Add to Quick List. You can get at the Quick List from the View menu.

To dial a number that isn't on your list, select View ➤ Dial Pad. Type in the number and click on Dial. Or if you need special characters such as a pause inserted in the number, click on Buttons>> to get a dial pad like the one shown in Figure 5.4.

contacting the programmer

Practical PhoneBook version 2.2a is copyrighted 1993-1994 by Gary Chizhevsky. To register, send $15 to:

Gary Chizhevsky
39821 Cedar Blvd., Apt. 109
Newark, CA 94560

◻ **FIGURE 5.4**
Use Dial Pad to
click on numbers
manually and
then dial.

Registration gets you free upgrades, technical support, and the knowledge that you're a decent human (at least in this respect). For information, to ask questions, or to offer suggestions, you can reach Gary at the following locations:

Voice: 510-656-7039
America OnLine: Murlo
Internet: murlo@aol.com

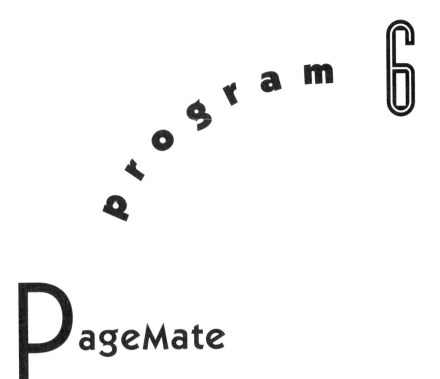

Program 6

PageMate

Years ago there was a popular form of entertainment known as the one-man band. This was a guy who could dazzle a crowd by playing half a dozen musical instruments at very high speed. What a piker, I hear you saying, only half a dozen? Most of us have to juggle multiple projects plus be in at least three places at the same time.

As you know, if you have to be out of your office a lot and still need to know when calls come in, you have a problem. You can hire a receptionist (using the piles of cash you have lying around) or you can economize and use PageMate. PageMate will call your pager and let you know when you've gotten a call. You can then call your answering machine and retrieve the message.

To use PageMate, you need to have a modem and your answering machine must be on the same phone line as the modem.

installing

It takes just a few steps to install PageMate:

1. Put Disk 2 in drive A. Open File Manager and click on the A drive icon.

2. Highlight the file PAGEMATE.EXE and then select File ➤ Copy from the File Manager menu. Copy the file to a temporary location on your hard disk.

3. Go to the directory where you've placed PAGEMATE.EXE and double-click on the file name. The files inside PAGE-MATE.EXE will be extracted.

TIP

If the files don't show up in the File Manager window after you extract them, press F5 to refresh the view. F5 also refreshes the drive window in Norton Desktop for Windows.

4. Double-click on the file SETUP.EXE and PageMate will install itself, pausing only to let you change the default directory should you want to do so. If the SETUP program finds duplicate files on your hard disk (this sometimes happens, particularly with .DLL files), it'll let you know. If SETUP's version of the file is newer (check the date) or larger, then let it overwrite the older file.

After installation is complete, delete all the files from the temporary location. These files aren't necessary to run the program and just take up hard disk space.

getting started

PageMate installs itself in its own group. All you have to do to get it started is double-click on the PageMate icon. This will open the window you see in Figure 6.1.

□ **FIGURE 6.1**
The PageMate
screen—a model of
simplicity

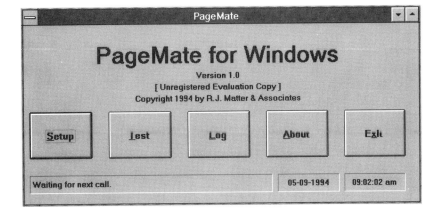

TIP

Don't be upset if you get a message that your modem isn't responding. We'll fix that while we're setting it up for your system.
Just click on Cancel and keep going.

When PageMate opens, click on the Setup button. This will open
the configuration screen shown in Figure 6.2.

□ **FIGURE 6.2**
This is where
you enter the
information
PageMate needs
in order to work.

Here's what all those boxes mean:

Com Port

The program assumes your modem is attached to Com1. If it's not, you got a scary message about your modem not responding. Click on the button for the correct port.

Baud Rate

The baud rate is only important in that you have to supply a baud rate to configure a serial port. So it doesn't matter which one you choose as long as it's no faster than your modem will support. Also, the baud rate has to be 1200 or faster for dial tone detection to work.

Line Service

The default is tone. Don't change it unless you know you have pulse line service.

Busy Redial

The default is for PageMate to redial if it gets a busy signal.

Transmit

Here's where you select the message you want to appear on your pager. The default is the number (presumably your office number) that you'll enter in the Transmit Number box below. Or click on the drop-down list arrow and select Time (to display the time the last call was received) or Counter (to show a count of the calls received).

Modem Initialization String

Leave this alone unless you know your modem requires some special command codes.

Delay Secs	This is the number of seconds you want PageMate to delay before calling the pager. The default is 180 seconds (three minutes), which should give even the most long-winded client time to leave a message.
Pager Number	Enter the number you want PageMate to call. You can include *70 to disable call waiting, and you can add commas (each one representing a two-second pause) if you need them.
Transmit Number	This is the number you want transmitted to your pager. End the number with a # sign or whatever character is required by your paging service to indicate completion of the call.
Hangup Secs	Here you indicate how long PageMate should wait before hanging up the line. Usually the default of 20 seconds is long enough, but you can increase the time if you wish.

Once you have everything entered, click on the Save button. To see if everything is working right, click on the Test button. Click on Exit when you're done.

Now whenever you need to leave the office, start PageMate and leave it open on the desktop. It will sit there patiently waiting for the phone to ring, and it won't cost you anything extra.

■ ■ ■ ■ ■ ■ ■ ■ ■ ■ ■ ■ ■ ■ ■ ■ ## other features

PageMate also keeps a log of calls in and out for you. Click on the Log button to view it. When you want to save or otherwise get rid of an overlong log, just save it under another name. The default name is PAGE.LOG.

■ ■ ■ ■ ■ ■ ■ ■ ■ ■ ## contacting the programmer

PageMate version 1.0 is copyrighted 1994 by R.J. Matter & Associates. You can register it by sending $35 to:

R.J. Matter
P.O. Box 9042
Highland, IN 46322-9042

Voice: 219-845-5247
CompuServe: 71021,2654

P A R T . . . .

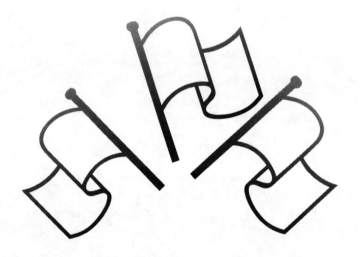

3

Getting Graphic

It's true that when you're in business for yourself, you have to be a Jack (or Jill) of all trades. So even if you can't draw a straight line with the aid of a ruler, at some point you'll probably be called upon to do something vaguely artistic. For example, you may have to convert or manipulate graphic images on your computer or produce a decent-looking chart. In this section you'll find some programs that will help even the most artistically impaired.

program 7

Chartist

I consider myself among the graphically challenged in this world. When my class had to draw charts or graphs in school, mine were not usually among the teachers' favorites. Maybe it was all the smeared eraser marks. Anyway, when computer drawing programs came along, I was among the first in line.

But even if your drawings are a work of art, a program like Chartist can be of tremendous help. You can experiment, change your mind, and try different looks, all without pain (or wasting stacks of drawing paper). You can print out as many copies as you want and issue updates at any time without having to do everything all over again.

Chartist gives you a very sophisticated array of tools for drawing charts in a package that's easy to learn and use.

■ **installing**

To install Chartist, just follow these steps:

1. Put Disk 1 in drive A. Open File Manager and click on the A drive icon.

2. Highlight the file CHARTS.EXE and then select File ➤ Copy from the File Manager menu. Copy the file to a temporary location on your hard disk.

3. Go to the directory where you've placed CHARTS.EXE and double-click on the file name. The files inside CHARTS.EXE will be extracted.

TIP

If the files don't show up in the File Manager window after you extract them, press F5 to refresh the view. The F5 key also refreshes the drive window in Norton Desktop for Windows.

4. Double-click on the file INSTALL.EXE and Chartist will install itself, pausing only to let you change the default directory should you want to do so.

5. You can run Chartist by double-clicking on CHARTIST.EXE (it'll be in the CHARTIST directory unless you specified another location). You can run Chartist from the .EXE file, install the program in an existing group, or make a new group.

After installation is complete, delete all the files from the temporary location. These files aren't necessary to run the program and just take up hard disk space.

■ ■ ■ ■ ■ ■ ■ ■ ■ ■ ■ ■ ■ ■ ■ ■ ■ ■ **getting started**

The opening screen for Chartist, shown in Figure 7.1, looks much like other drawing programs (except for the grid) and is about as

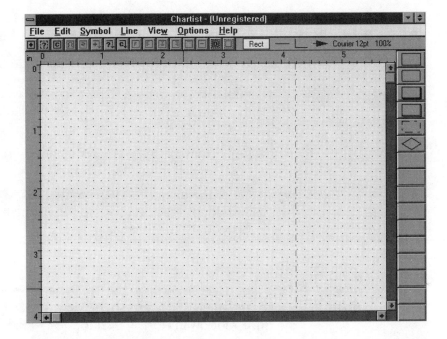

helpful. But after you poke around for a few minutes, you'll feel quite at home.

In addition to the menus and toolbar on the top of the screen, you'll see a status bar to the right. Down the right side of the screen are the default shapes. You can add shapes to this default palette by pressing F4 or by selecting Symbol ➤ Shape. Click on the name of a shape and preview it in the box to the right. Click on Add to Palette and the symbol will appear on the next available button.

TIP
To see what commands are attached to each button on the toolbar, press F1 when you're in the main Chartist window. Choose the Toolbar topic.

To put a symbol on your chart, click on the button with the symbol. Then click on the spot where you want the symbol to appear.

To add text to a symbol, double-click on it. This will open the Edit Symbol Text box shown in Figure 7.2. Type in the text you want and then click on OK.

TIP

The Edit Symbol Text box doesn't provide word-wrap. If you want all the text to be inside the symbol, you'll have to press Enter at the end of each line.

◘ **FIGURE 7.2**
The Edit Symbol
Text box

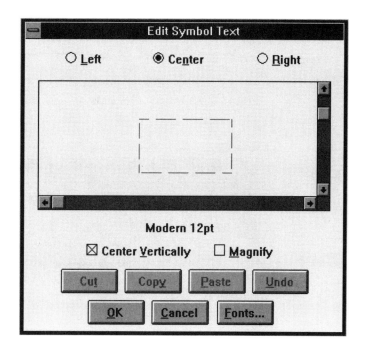

making a chart

Here's how to make a simple chart:

1. Click on a shape button once. Then click on the spot where you want the shape to appear.

2. Double-click on the shape to open the Edit Symbol Text box.

3. Click on Fonts to select one of the fonts in your system. Type in the text you want, and then click OK.

4. Repeat step 3 to add another shape and the text to go with it.

5. Connect the shapes by pressing the Tab key. Move the mouse to the spot where you want to start the line. A pencil shape will appear. (It takes some practice to get the technique right.)

6. Click the mouse at the starting point and drag the line to the spot where you want it to end.

Figure 7.3 shows a chart made very quickly using just these simple tools.

□ **FIGURE 7.3**
A beginner's chart

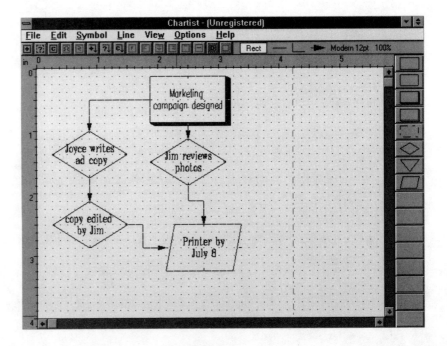

Practically everything on a chart can be customized. You can change the look of the lines (Line ➤ Style) or you can add a pattern to a symbol (Symbol ➤ Hatch Pattern). You can also add colors and pictures as well as designate the chart size.

The key in most of the customizing is to click on the symbol first, then choose what you want to do with it.

When you're all done, select File ➤ Print to print a copy of your chart. Or save the chart (File ➤ Save) to work on it again another day.

Some sample charts are included with Chartist. Figure 7.4 shows RELATE.CHT, one possible chart variation.

□ **FIGURE 7.4**
A chart drawn with curved lines (using Line ➤ Style)

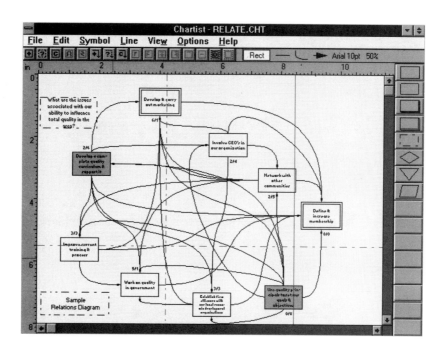

contacting the programmer

Chartist is copyrighted 1991-1993 by Novagraph, Inc. Registration is $79 (plus $3 for shipping in the U.S. and $6 elsewhere). When you register, you'll get a printed manual, the latest version of the software, and technical support for a year. You'll also get an additional library of more than 100 shapes and arrowheads.

There's also an enhanced version called Chartist-2 that has more features; it costs $125 plus shipping.

Send the registration fee to:

Novagraph, Inc.
P.O. Box 850115
Richardson, TX 75085-0115

Voice: 214-231-2169
Fax: 214-235-0607

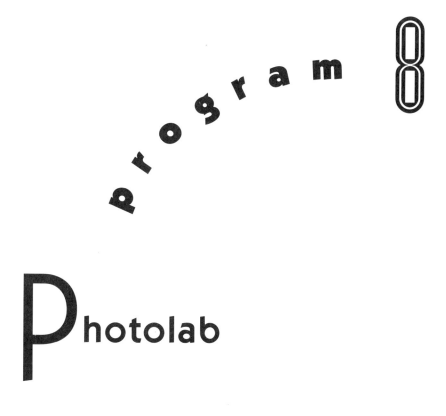

Program 8

Photolab

Almost any flyer, newsletter, advertisement, or promotional piece looks better with the addition of a graphic or two. The problem with computer graphics, as you may have discovered, is that there are so many formats! So when you find the perfect graphic for your newsletter, you inevitably discover that your word processor won't work with that particular format. Or perhaps you have an image and the size isn't quite right, or some of the colors need to be changed. Install Photolab and put it to work for you.

■   **installing**

You can install Photolab in just a few steps:

1. Put Disk 2 in drive A. Open File Manager and click on the A drive icon.

2. Highlight the file PHOTO.EXE and then select File ➤ Copy from the File Manager menu. Copy the file to a temporary location on your hard disk.

3. Go to the directory where you've placed PHOTO.EXE and double-click on the file name. The files inside PHOTO.EXE will be extracted.

TIP

If the files don't show up in the File Manager window after you extract them, press F5 to refresh the view. F5 also refreshes the drive window in Norton Desktop for Windows.

4. Double-click on the file INSTALL.EXE. If you *don't* want the program to have its own group inside Program Manager, click on the Add Icons to Program Manager box to remove the check mark. When that box is clear, the program will still be installed in its own directory, but you'll have to run it by double-clicking on the .EXE program from a File Manager window. This only makes sense if the program is to be used very rarely.

5. If you want the program to be in your StartUp group, make sure that box is checked. Then click on OK.

6. If the INSTALL program finds duplicate files on your hard disk (this sometimes happens, particularly with .DLL files), it'll let you know. If the INSTALL version of the file is newer (check the date) or larger, then let it overwrite the older file.

After installation is complete, delete all the files from the temporary location. These files aren't necessary to run the program and just take up hard disk space.

getting started

When you have an image you want to manipulate, double-click on the Photolab icon. Select File ➤ Open and supply the name and location of the image.

Figure 8.1 shows a familiar-looking bitmap called EARTH.BMP that I opened in Photolab. It was considerably smaller than this when it was first loaded, so I selected Zoom ➤ 300% to get a more workable view. That's why you can see so many individual pixels.

TIP

You can also zoom in by clicking on the image once with the left mouse button. Zoom out by clicking the right mouse button.

◘ FIGURE 8.1
The bitmap EARTH.BMP expanded by 300 percent

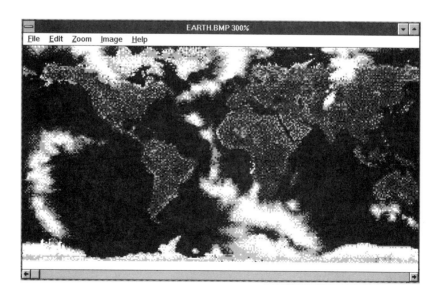

To get a different perspective, I tried Image ➤ Mirror and got the not-at-all-familiar look you see in Figure 8.2.

■ **FIGURE 8.2**
The mirror image
of EARTH.BMP

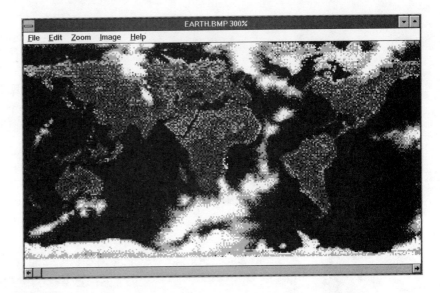

You can also rotate the image 90 degrees to the right or left, flip it, turn a positive into a negative, or vice versa. Photolab lets you adjust the color tone of an image by selecting Image ➤ Adjust. This opens the Adjust window shown in Figure 8.3. Slide the scroll boxes here and there to get the effect you want.

getting great effects

Photolab includes some pretty sophisticated graphic manipulation tools. For example, you can add any of a dozen or so filters to any image by selecting Image ➤ Filters. The box that opens, shown in Figure 8.4, provides a list of ready-made filters on the right. Or you can enter your own values and save them under a new name.

Save your changed image by selecting File ➤ Save, or save it in a completely new format by choosing Save As instead.

◻ FIGURE 8.3
The scroll bars let you fine-tune the image's color, brightness, and other qualities.

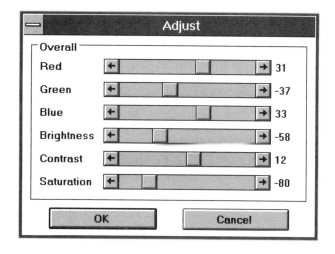

◻ FIGURE 8.4
A list of filters you can use on an image

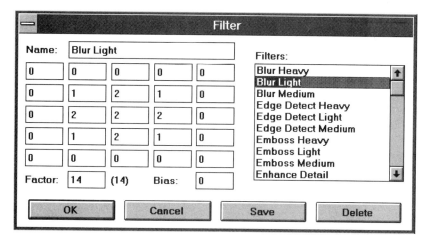

TIP

If you have a Hewlett-Packard color scanner, you can scan in a picture and use Photolab to modify it. Just choose File ➤ Scan and then set the size and resolution you want.

▪ ▪ ▪ ▪ ▪ ▪ ▪ ▪ ▪ ▪ contacting the programmer

Photolab version 1.8a is copyrighted 1993 by Daniel S. Baker. Registration is a modest $30 and will gain you an authorized copy of Photolab on diskette as well as free upgrades when available. Send your registration fee to:

Daniel S. Baker
5993 Slippery Rock Drive
Columbus, OH 43229

You can also reach Dan on CompuServe (71551,2300), where he cheerfully answers questions. He's quite happy to get requests for enhancements and any reports of difficulties you may have.

FontSpec Pro

Fonts are one of those things you just can't have too many of—until you have *way* too many of them. I've never been able to resist adding just one or two more fonts to my system. Of course, when you have so many fonts you end up just using two or three because it's too much trouble to scan through a zillion fonts to find just the right one. FontSpec Pro comes to the rescue of font junkies, performing three functions in one package. With it you can:

- ◘ View installed and uninstalled fonts easily
- ◘ Print font specimen sheets
- ◘ Install and organize your fonts in an orderly way

You'll be able to sort through your fonts, organize them efficiently, and perhaps get rid of some of the ones you rarely use.

∎ ∎ ∎ ∎ ∎ ∎ ∎ ∎ ∎ ∎ ∎ ∎ ∎ ∎ ∎ ∎ ∎ ∎ ∎ **installing**

To install FontSpec Pro, just follow these steps:

1. Put Disk 2 in drive A. Open File Manager and click on the A drive icon.

2. Highlight the file FONTSPEC.EXE and then select File ➤ Copy from the File Manager menu. Copy the file to a temporary location on your hard disk.

3. Go to the directory where you've placed FONTSPEC.EXE and double-click on the file name. The files inside FONT-SPEC.EXE will be extracted.

TIP

If the files don't show up in the File Manager window after you extract them, press F5 to refresh the view. F5 also refreshes the drive window in Norton Desktop for Windows.

4. Double-click on the file FS-SETUP.EXE and you'll see the Install screen shown in Figure 9.1. If you want to change the directory to which FontSpec Pro will be installed, do so now and then click on the Install button. FontSpec Pro will quickly install itself and then present you with a whole group of icons, as shown in Figure 9.2.

∎ ∎ ∎ ∎ ∎ ∎ ∎ ∎ ∎ ∎ ∎ ∎ ∎ ∎ ∎ ∎ ∎ ∎ **getting started**

Click on the FontSpec Launcher icon to start FontSpec Pro. You will get a Launcher bar that looks like this:

◻ FIGURE 9.1
FontSpec Pro's install window shows the source and destination directories for installation.

◻ FIGURE 9.2
FontSpec Pro group window. Click on FontSpec Launcher to get started.

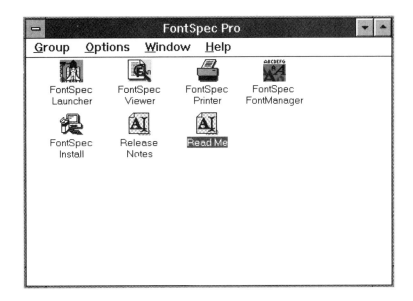

You can click on the edge of this bar and drag it to any spot on your screen that you find convenient. Wherever you put the Launcher bar, it will always be on top, so tuck it away in an accessible but unobtrusive spot on your desktop.

viewer

The Viewer is a good place to start because it makes no changes to your system, so you can experiment all you want. If you have the Launcher bar open on the desktop, you can click on the Viewer button to open the window shown in Figure 9.3. Another way to load the Viewer is by double-clicking on the FontSpec Viewer icon in the group window. As you move your mouse around, a helpful line appears just above the main text window (which FontSpec Pro calls the "viewport") describing each button.

◘ **FIGURE 9.3**
The Viewer window. Point to any spot on the window and a descriptive help line appears above the main text window.

Viewer Setup   Click on the Set-Up button to change the default settings. For example, if you have a number of bitmapped fonts and want them to be included in the list, select All Fonts in the View Fonts box. But be forewarned that bitmapped fonts will look very jagged at the larger font sizes. TrueType fonts will be smooth at any size. If you want a display of some particular line of text, type it in the User Defined Type Specimen box.

When the Viewer first opens, it shows just one font. If you want to see multiple lines at startup, select Off for the Startup Zoom option. However, showing more than one font at a time will be slow on older computers (386-33 and below).

Click on Done when you're—oh, I guess you can figure *that* out.

Font Viewing   To get a quick scan of one font after another, check the Multiple Lines box on the main Viewer screen. That way you can see a series of fonts very quickly, as shown in Figure 9.4.

◻ **FIGURE 9.4**
Check the Multiple Lines box to see a whole series of fonts quickly.

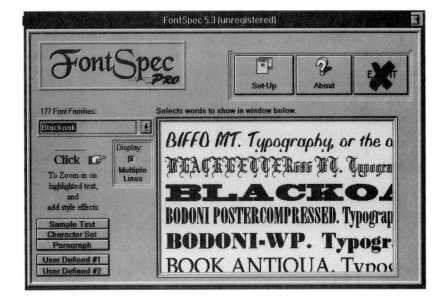

Use the ↑ and ↓ keys to find a font you like. Then remove the check from the Multiple Lines box and you can get the whole character set, a paragraph, or sample text, depending on which button you select.

printer

The Printer part of FontSpec Pro produces very nice, customizable font specimen sheets. To run the Printer module, click on the Launcher bar's Printer button. You can move the mouse around to get help, just as you would in the Viewer.

Setup Click on the Set-up button before you try to do any printing. You'll get the screen shown in Figure 9.5.

◻ FIGURE 9.5
Make your setup choices before printing specimen sheets.

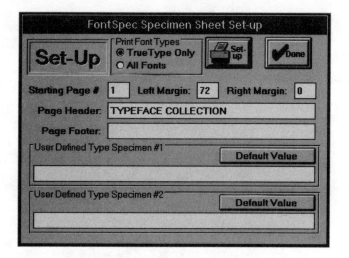

Starting Page # defaults to 1. You can set a different starting page number if you're printing sections and want to begin with a number other than 1. The printing starts with the first font selected regardless of the page number you enter.

The left and right margin settings range from 0 to 99 points (72 points equals one inch). The left margin default is 72, but you can change it to suit your preference.

The Page Header prints at the top of each page and the Page Footer prints at the bottom. Just as in the Viewer, you can supply your own text for the two User Defined Type Specimen boxes.

TIP

The unregistered version of FontSpec Pro doesn't allow you to choose a printer and print orientation as the registered version does. You can get around this problem by using the normal Windows method (double-click on Printers in the Control Panel in the Main group). This, however, doesn't absolve you of your responsibility to register!

Selecting Fonts to Print   FontSpec Pro lets you choose from different font lists. The first is Installed Fonts. These are all the fonts that are specified in your WIN.INI file; they're listed under Fonts in the Windows Control Panel. The other list is called Uninstalled Fonts although it actually includes *all* the fonts on your hard disk, whether they are installed in Windows or not.

When you print from the Installed Fonts list, you get a sample of the text (or a paragraph, or your own user-defined text) with the font name and size printed directly underneath. Printing from the Uninstalled Fonts list gives you the same example *plus* the file name of the font and its exact location on your disk.

Select either Installed or Uninstalled fonts. Click on the font name in the left column and that font will be added to the list on the right. Whoops! Picked one you don't want? Just click once on the name in the right column and it's removed. The Quick View window shows you a sample as each font is selected. Click on the Print button when you've made your selections.

You may want to experiment with a few sample pages to get the right point size and format before committing yourself to printing all your fonts in specimen sheets.

TIP

Printing out pages with 20 or more fonts on each one would push the capabilities of most printers to the limit. If you have a problem (random errors of various kinds), first make sure that you have the latest and greatest printer driver for your printer. Contact the manufacturer to make sure. If your laser printer still seems per-plexed, try switching to the HP Series II driver that came on your Windows disks. The Series II printer driver seems to work better with fonts even with a Laserjet III or Laserjet 4. It's faster, too.

font manager

The Font Manager is really a full-fledged application all by itself. It's a wonderful tool for sorting through all those fonts on your hard disk and organizing them into useful groups—not to mention getting rid of some of the dead-weight fonts that are just taking up perfectly good hard disk space!

Comparing Fonts   As you've no doubt discovered, a number of fonts that are really the same are roaming around masquerading under different names. For example, I had a font on my disk called Times New Roman and one called TimesNewRoman and one called Tms Rmn—and they were identical. To get rid of these deadbeats, click on the Font Manager button on the Launcher bar or double-click on the FontSpec FontManager icon in the FontSpec Pro group window. You'll get a window like the one shown in Figure 9.6.

◘ **FIGURE 9.6**
The Font Manager lets you get a grip on the many fonts you've accumulated.

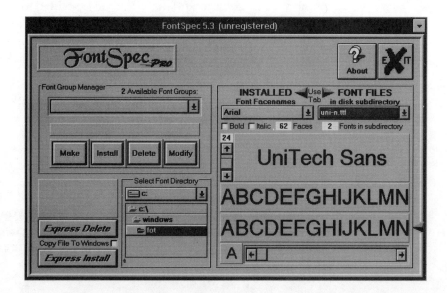

In the Select Font Directory list box, select the directory where the suspect fonts hang out. Use the two list boxes to select an installed font and a font file (installed or not). A sample of each will be displayed below the lists. This area is scrollable, so you can compare the two fonts throughout the entire character set. An arrow on the right points to the current font; use the Tab key to toggle back and forth.

When FontSpec Pro detects that the two fonts are more or less identical, both sample lines will automatically be highlighted.

Express Install and Express Delete   To install a font file, click on Express Install to immediately install the font being pointed to in Windows. If you check the Copy File to Windows box, the font file will be copied to the Windows directory; otherwise it will be installed based on its current location. (That means if you later move it, Windows will not be able to find it again.)

To get rid of an extraneous font, use the Tab key to move the pointer to the font you want to get rid of and then click on the Express Delete button.

WARNING

Be careful using Express Delete. This one button click will not only remove the font from Windows (if it's installed), it will also remove the font from your hard disk. That's it. Gone.

Grouping Fonts   For those of us with lots of fonts, FontSpec Pro's ability to organize fonts into groups is a real timesaver. For example, if you have a selection of fonts that you use for a newsletter, put these fonts in their own group and you can have them all at your fingertips when you need them. Or you may have a selection that you use only for a particular client. Put them in their own group and you won't have to look around for them when the need arises.

To make a group, follow these steps:

1. Click on the Make button. When making your first group, you'll be asked whether you want to save your current

Windows configuration in case you ever want to go back to it. Go ahead and do it.

2. Select the drive and directory that hold your fonts.

3. Click once on the file name to see a sample of the font in the Quick View window. Double-click on the font name and it'll be added to the Font Group list box.

4. You can add more fonts from other directories by navigating to the directory and adding the fonts as described in step 3.

5. When you're finished with the group, type in an appropriate name in the Group Name box and click on Done.

Figure 9.7 shows a group I created to hold all the oddball fonts on my hard drive.

□ FIGURE 9.7
The font group Weird Stuff isolates all the strange fonts that I need very rarely.

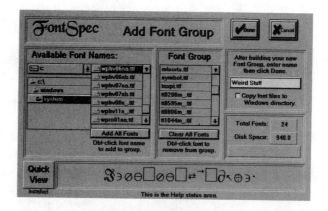

When you want to use a particular group of fonts, open Font Manager and click on the Available Font Groups drop-down list box. Select a font group and click on Install. In a minute or less, the group will be installed and available to Windows. Open a Windows application and your fonts will be listed (so will any printer fonts and system fonts as well as any non-TrueType fonts that are already installed).

You can delete a font group by selecting it and then clicking on the Delete button. This will delete the group but leave your actual font files intact (unlike the very hazardous-to-your-fonts Express Delete button, which erases them completely).

TIP

The README.TXT file that comes with FontSpec Pro includes a good description of how to consolidate your TrueType fonts into one directory, which saves a lot of time and energy when you back up your files. Search for the heading "A Sample Session."

contacting the programmer

FontSpec Pro version 5.3 is copyrighted 1993 by UniTech Corporation. At the heart of UniTech is Nick Naimo, who provides cheerful and helpful tech support to everyone who calls—registered user or not!

Registration is only $25, which makes this very useful program one of the best bargains in this book. You can use your MasterCard or Visa to make it even more convenient. To register, send a check to the address below or call to place a credit card order:

UniTech Corporation
2697 McKelvey Road
Maryland Heights, MO 63043
Voice: 314-770-2770

program 10

FontLine

FontLine is not one of the bigger packages featured in this book. It simply lets you take some text, modify it in several ways, and then save it as an image. Specifically, a bitmapped image.

The bitmap produced by FontLine can be placed in any document that you send on disk or transmit by modem. When it's printed out, it will look exactly as you designed it—even if the receiving party doesn't possess the fonts you used in creating the image.

In other words, FontLine may be small, but it packs a punch.

Keep this program iconized and handy while using Windows Write or Paintbrush and you'll add more capability to both applications. You can use a Dingbats font to create borders, make customized letterheads, add colorful and attention-grabbing entries to your word-processing documents, or rotate text and plug it into a Paintbrush creation.

installing

There are two ways to install FontLine.

first method

Use the first method if you expect to use the program fairly often:

1. Put Disk 1 in drive A. Open File Manager and click on the A drive icon.

2. Highlight the file FNTLINE.EXE and then select File ➤ Copy from the File Manager menu. Copy the file to a temporary location on your hard disk.

3. Go to the directory where you've placed FNTLINE.EXE and double-click on the file name. The files inside FNTLINE.EXE will be extracted.

TIP

If the files don't show up in the File Manager window after you extract them, press F5 to refresh the view. F5 also refreshes the drive window in Norton Desktop for Windows.

4. Double-click on the file INSTALL.EXE.

5. If you want the program to be in your StartUp group, make sure that box is checked. Then click on OK.

6. If the INSTALL program finds duplicate files on your hard disk (this sometimes happens, particularly with .DLL files), it'll let you know. If the INSTALL version of the file is newer (check the date) or larger, then let it overwrite the older file.

After installation is complete, delete all the files from the temporary location. These files aren't necessary to run the program and just take up hard disk space.

second method

If you don't expect to use FontLine more than occasionally, you can install it this way:

1. Make a directory called FONTLINE on your hard drive.

2. Put Disk 1 in drive A. Open File Manager and click on the A drive icon.

3. Highlight the file FNTLINE.EXE and then select File ➤ Copy from the File Manager menu. Copy the file to FONTLINE (or any other directory you choose).

4. Go to the directory where you've placed FNTLINE.EXE and double-click on the file name. The files inside FNTLINE.EXE will be extracted.

TIP

If the files don't show up in the File Manager window after you extract them, press F5 to refresh the view. F5 also refreshes the drive window in Norton Desktop for Windows.

5. When you want to use FontLine, open File Manager and select the FONTLINE directory. Double-click on FNTLINE.EXE to start the program.

getting started

When you start the program, you'll get a very basic-looking box that says "Text." To put in the words you want, click on Text in the menu bar. This will give you the dialog box shown in Figure 10.1.

You can adjust the following settings:

◻ **Text Angle (degrees)** Tilt the text this number of degrees. The angle counts counterclockwise, though negative values are allowed.

◘ **FIGURE 10.1**
Type in the text you want as well as the desired angle, width, and spacing.

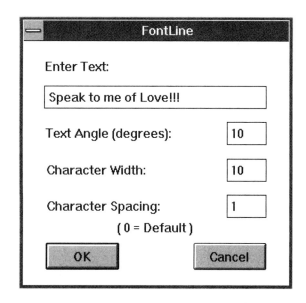

Click on OK when you have these settings right. Next, select the Font Menu item. You'll be able to pick from among all the scalable fonts installed.

◘ **Character Width** This will change the width of the characters.

◘ **Character Spacing** Type in a higher number to increase the amount of space between each character. Negative values move the characters closer together.

Click on OK when you have these settings right. Next, select the Font Menu item. You'll be able to pick from among all the scalable fonts installed.

Resize the window to get the right size. You'll probably want to make the window as small as possible. Figure 10.2 shows the result of the selections shown in Figure 10.1 using the font Lucida Calligraphy.

Click on Copy and the text will be copied to the Clipboard as a bitmap. Open the application where you want to put the bitmap and then select Paste from the Edit menu; Figure 10.3 shows an example.

◘ **FIGURE 10.2**
Now I've chosen a font and made the window as small as possible so that the bitmap won't have too much blank space.

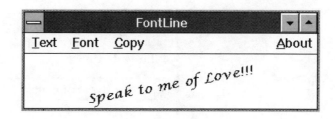

◘ **FIGURE 10.3**
Inserted in a Windows Write document, this file will look the same on any system— even those without the Lucida Calligraphy font.

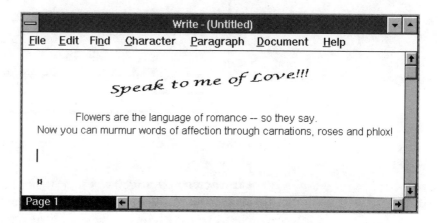

contacting the programmer

FontLine is freeware offered by its author, Gordon D. Griffiths of Kanata, Canada. Your only obligation in using this program is to occasionally think a kind thought about Mr. Griffiths and wish him well. I certainly do.

P A R T . . . .

4

Take a Letter!

Letters and other mailings are part of everyday life in a business. Getting your grammar straight—not to mention printing envelopes and labels—can be a persistent problem. In this section, you'll find three programs that will help you communicate with the outside world with maximum efficiency.

Program 11

Grammar Expert

Lots of word processors come with a grammar checker. But running your document through some of these programs is like putting sirloin through a meat grinder: What comes out the other end is barely recognizable. And if you are hoity-toity enough to use words of more than one syllable, the program chastises you for being an elitist!

Grammar Expert is not like that. In fact, it becomes part of your Windows help files and stands by modestly waiting to be called on. When you have a question about correct usage or punctuation, click on the Grammar Expert icon and you get lots of helpful information—and no lectures about your writing style!

▪ **installing**

1. Put Disk 1 in drive A. Open File Manager and click on the A drive icon.

2. Highlight the file GRAMEXP.EXE and then select File ➤ Copy from the File Manager menu. Copy the file to a temporary location on your hard disk.

3. Go to the directory where you've placed GRAMEXP.EXE and double-click on the file name. The files inside GRAMEXP.EXE will be extracted.

TIP

If the files don't show up in the File Manager window after you extract them, press F5 to refresh the view. F5 also refreshes the drive window in Norton Desktop for Windows.

4. Double-click on the file INSTALL.EXE. If you *don't* want the program to have its own group inside Program Manager, click on the Add Icons to Program Manager box to remove the check mark. When that box is clear, the program will still be installed in its own directory, but you'll have to run it by double-clicking on the .EXE program from a File Manager window.

5. If you want the program to be in your StartUp group, make sure that box is checked. Then click on OK.

6. If the INSTALL program finds duplicate files on your hard disk (this sometimes happens, particularly with .DLL files), it'll let you know. If the INSTALL version of the file is newer (check the date) or larger, then let it overwrite the older file.

After installation is complete, delete all the files from the temporary location. These files aren't necessary to run the program and just take up hard disk space.

TIP

If you decide to put Grammar Expert in the StartUp group after you've installed it, enable the Run Minimized option in the Properties dialog box for Grammar Expert. This will run the program as an icon at the bottom of your screen.

getting started

To get acquainted with Grammar Expert, double-click on the icon to start it up. To see the table of contents, click on the words "Click here to continue" at the bottom of the page. This will open the window shown in Figure 11.1. Click on the line that says "Detailed table of contents." The words in green (light gray in the figure) are

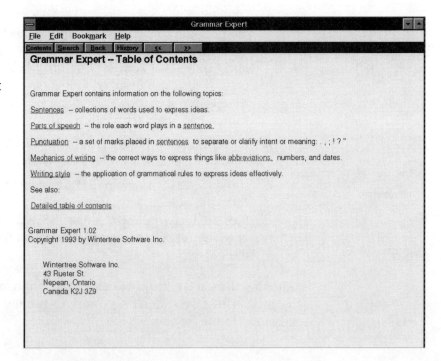

called "hypertext links." These links let you jump around to find answers quickly. Click on any one of these to get more information.

Just double-click on the Grammar Expert icon when you find yourself perplexed over a question of English usage. Select the Search button and type in the first few letters of the subject you want to investigate. Figure 11.2 shows the window that opens on the subject of dependent clauses.

◻ **FIGURE 11.2**
Grammar Expert's take on dependent clauses

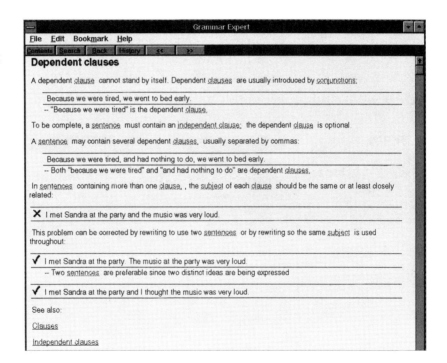

◻ ◻ ◻ ◻ ◻ ◻ ◻ ◻ ◻ ◻ ◻ ◻ ◻ ◻ ◻ ◻ ◻ **customizing**

Like every other program in the world, Grammar Expert lets you adjust certain settings to make the program just right for you.

always on top

When you minimize Grammar Expert, you may find that it gets lost behind your word processor or other programs. To make the icon always pop up on top of *whatever's* running, select Always on Top from Grammar Expert's Help menu.

add your own notes

You can add your own notes and associate them with a page. When the Grammar Expert page is visible, select Edit ➤ Annotate. Type in your notes and click on OK when you're done. A small paper clip icon will display next to the page's title, as shown in Figure 11.3. Just click on the paper clip icon to see your notes.

□ **FIGURE 11.3**
The paper clip icon indicates that there are notes associated with this page.

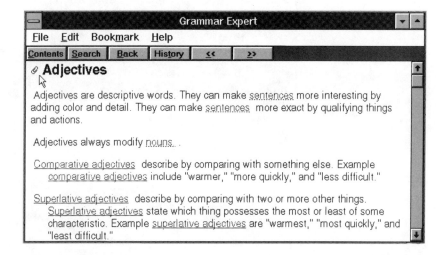

set colors

Grammar Expert uses both "jumps," which are links to related pages, and "popups," which are links to subwindows containing definitions. By default, Windows shows everything that has a link in green text. If you want, you can specify different colors. Here's how:

1. Make a backup copy of your WIN.INI file (just in case).

2. Using Notepad, open the file WIN.INI.

3. Look for a section called [Windows Help]. In that section, insert lines like

   Jumpcolor=red green blue
   Popupcolor=red green blue

   The numbers represent the amount of red, green, and blue color to use on a scale from 0 (none) to 255 (maximum). To make jump words red, for example, you would type in

   Jumpcolor=255 0 0

4. Save the file and restart Windows for the change to take effect.

TIP

If there's no section called [Windows Help] in your WIN.INI file, just add one at the end of the file. Make sure to include the square brackets ([]).

contacting the programmer

Grammar Expert version 1.02 is copyrighted 1992 by Wintertree Software, Inc., and costs $30 to register. To make it worth your while, registration will get you the latest version of Grammar Expert (without the "nag" screen), the next upgrade for free, and a free copy of Wintertree Software's *Guide to Frequently Confused Words*. This guide installs on your computer and is very handy.

You can register by sending a check for $30 (U.S.) to:

Wintertree Software, Inc.
43 Rueter Street
Nepean, Ontario
Canada K2J 3Z9
Voice: 613-825-6271

Credit card orders can be placed with the Public Software Library (PSL) at 1-800-242-4PSL, by fax at 713-524-6398, or by sending CompuServe email to 71355,470. These PSL numbers are for orders only. For help with questions and tech support, you'll need to get in touch with the folks in Canada.

Program 12

PostMaster

If you find that, despite the investment of thousands of dollars in high-tech equipment, you're still hauling out a typewriter to address individual envelopes, PostMaster is the program for you. Print one envelope or many. You can use any fonts on your system and customize the look of your envelopes very quickly without even opening a word-processing program.

PostMaster, like the other programs in this book, is terrifically easy to use. There are only a few options for you to set and you're ready to go.

■ ■ ■ ■ ■ ■ ■ ■ ■ ■ ■ ■ ■ ■ ■ ■ ■ ■ ■ **installing**

Just follow these steps to install PostMaster:

1. Open File Manager and look in your WINDOWS\SYS-TEM directory for the file VBRUN300.DLL. If you see the file in this directory, jump ahead to step 3. If you don't see it, put Disk 1 in drive A and copy the file VBRUN3.EXE to the WINDOWS\SYSTEM directory.

2. Double-click on VBRUN3.EXE and the file VBRUN300.DLL will be extracted. (You can then delete VBRUN3.EXE to save space.)

3. Place Disk 2 in drive A. Open File Manager and click on the A drive icon.

4. Highlight the file POST.EXE and then select File ➤ Copy from the File Manager menu. Copy the file to a temporary location on your hard disk.

5. Go to the directory where you've placed POST.EXE and double-click on the file name. The files inside POST.EXE will be extracted.

TIP

If the files don't show up in the File Manager window after you extract them, press F5 to refresh the view. F5 also refreshes the drive window in Norton Desktop for Windows.

6. Double-click on the file INSTALL.EXE and you'll see a window like the one shown in Figure 12.1.

7. If you *don't* want the program to have its own group inside Program Manager, click on the Add Icons to Program Manager box to remove the check mark. When that box is clear, the program will still be installed in its own directory, but you'll have to run it by double-clicking on

◻ FIGURE 12.1
The PostMaster
Install window

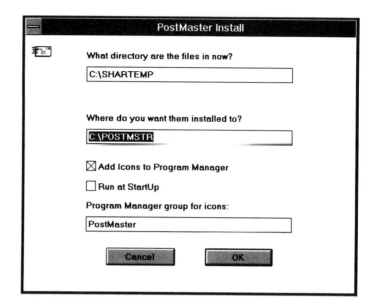

the .EXE program from a File Manager window. This only makes sense if you plan to use the program very rarely.

8. If you want the program to be in your StartUp group, make sure that box is checked. Then click on OK.

9. If the INSTALL program finds duplicate files on your hard disk (this sometimes happens, particularly with .DLL files), it'll let you know. If the INSTALL version of the file is newer (check the date) or larger than the one already on your hard disk, then let the program overwrite the older file.

After installation is complete, delete all the files from the temporary location. These files aren't necessary to run the program and just take up hard disk space.

TIP

If you decide to put PostMaster in the StartUp group after you've installed it, enable the Run Minimized option in the Properties

dialog box for PostMaster. This will run the program as an icon at the bottom of your screen.

getting started

Double-click on the PostMaster icon to get the (mostly) self-explanatory window shown in Figure 12.2. At the simplest level, you can just type in the addressee plus your return address and then click on the Print with Laser button. Of course, there are lots of other things you can do.

□ **FIGURE 12.2**
The PostMaster window with some addresses supplied

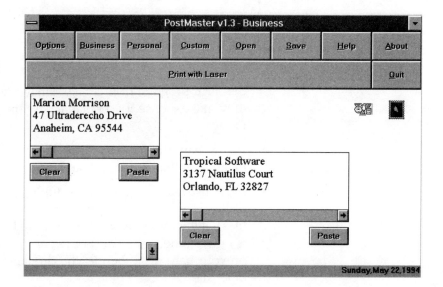

envelope size

Set the envelope size by clicking on Business, Personal, or Custom. Business, the default, is the standard #10 envelope, 4⅛ by 9½ inches. Personal means an envelope that's 3⅝ by 6½ inches. For other sizes, click on Custom and specify the dimensions in inches.

fonts

Click on the Options button and select either Change Return Address Font or Change Address Font. Unlike some word processors, with PostMaster you can specify different fonts for each address and save them that way too.

saving addresses

To save an address for future use, click on the Save button. Supply a name for the saved address, as shown in Figure 12.3, and click on OK.

◘ **FIGURE 12.3**
Saving the address for tropical software

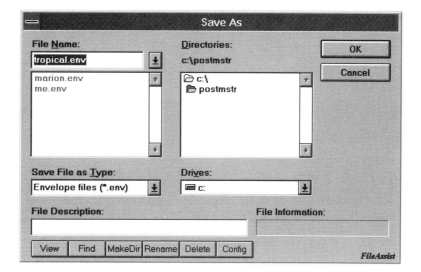

retrieving saved addresses

To open an address that you've previously saved, click on the Open button. In the window that pops up, highlight any file on the list and the contents will appear in the lower right corner; see Figure 12.4 for an example. This very neat feature lets you quickly determine exactly whose address you saved as BOB.ENV.

◘ **FIGURE 12.4**
The contents of
each .ENV file are
displayed when
you click on the
file name.

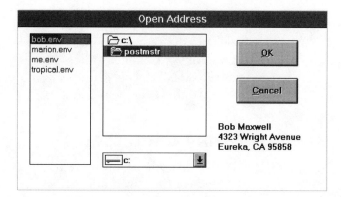

saving and retrieving return addresses

Because PostMaster saves all addresses in the same format, you
need to specify which address to save (the one in the return window) and where to place the retrieved address (also in the return
window). Do this by selecting the appropriate Save or Retrieve in-
struction from the Options menu.

printer setup

PostMaster uses the default printer as specified in your Windows
Control Panel. You won't need to change anything under Printer
Setup (Options menu) unless your printer isn't working properly.

Click the Help button and select Operation and then Print to get
assistance.

TIP

**The drop-down list box in the lower left corner of the "envelope"
gives you a choice of special notations such as "Personal" or
"Fragile" that can be imprinted as well.**

mailing list

In addition to simple one-at-a-time envelopes, you can also set up multiple address files. To make your own mailing lists, select Options ➤ Mailing List and then follow these steps:

1. Click on the Add button. The list of saved addresses will open.

2. Click on an address name and then the OK button. The address will be added to the list in the mailing list window. Highlight a name and click on the Remove button to take it off the list.

3. When your list is complete, click on Save. You'll be prompted for a name. After you type in the name, click on OK.

To print envelopes from a mailing list, follow these steps:

1. Select Options ➤ Mailing List.

2. Click on the Open button.

3. Click on Print and an envelope will be printed for each address on the list.

WARNING

When you make changes or additions to a previously saved mailing list and click on the Save button, the changes will be incorporated automatically. PostMaster will not prompt you to be sure this is what you want to do, so be careful!

contacting the programmer

PostMaster version 1.3 is copyrighted 1993 by Mark Jesiel. Registration is a very modest $10 and entitles you to technical support and notification of future upgrades. You'll also get a registration number that will get rid of the reminder screen you see when signing off.

Mark is happy to respond to suggestions, comments, and questions via CompuServe. Send the registration fee to the following address (include your CompuServe ID if you have one):

Tropical Software
3137 Nautilus Court
Orlando, FL 32827
CompuServe: 71554,3102

Program 13

ViaPrint

As mentioned earlier, I am definitely among the artistically un-skilled of the world—I very nearly failed finger-painting in kinder-garten. And yet the promotional material that comes out of my office—mailings, flyers, business cards—all needs to look compe-tent and professional. A very useful tool in this regard is the share-ware program ViaPrint.

ViaPrint lets you print custom-designed mailing labels of every kind, including all the usual sizes of Avery laser labels preset for you. You can also do quite a bit of design, including flyers and busi-ness cards, with nothing but ViaPrint and a decent-quality printer.

■ **installing**

Install ViaPrint by following these steps:

1. Open File Manager and look in your WINDOWS\SYS-TEM directory for the file VBRUN300.DLL. If you see the file in this directory, jump ahead to step 3. If you don't see it, put Disk 1 in drive A and copy the file VBRUN3.EXE to the WINDOWS\SYSTEM directory.

2. Double-click on VBRUN3.EXE and the file VBRUN300.DLL will be extracted. (You can then delete VBRUN3.EXE to save space.)

3. Place Disk 2 in drive A. Open File Manager and click on the A drive icon.

4. Highlight the file VPRINT.EXE and then select File ➤ Copy from the File Manager menu. Copy the file to a temporary location on your hard disk.

5. Go to the directory where you've placed VPRINT.EXE and double-click on the file name. The files inside VPRINT.EXE will be extracted.

TIP

If the files don't show up in the File Manager window after you extract them, press F5 to refresh the view. F5 also refreshes the drive window in Norton Desktop for Windows.

6. Double-click on the file INSTALL.EXE to start the installation program.

7. If you *don't* want ViaPrint to have its own group inside Program Manager, click on the Add Icons to Program Manager box to remove the check mark. When that box is clear, the program will still be installed in its own directory, but you'll have to run it by double-clicking on the .EXE program from a File Manager window. This only makes sense if you plan to use the program very rarely.

8. If you want the program to be in your StartUp group, make sure that box is checked. Then click on OK.

9. If the INSTALL program finds duplicate files on your hard disk (this sometimes happens, particularly with .DLL files), it'll let you know. If the INSTALL version of the file is newer (check the date) or larger than the one already on your hard disk, then let the program overwrite the older file.

After installation is complete, delete all the files from the temporary location. These files aren't necessary to run the program and just take up hard disk space.

some basic concepts

With ViaPrint, you choose the size of the label (or flyer, or whatever) and then add Text Boxes, Angle Boxes (Text Boxes that can be rotated), Line Boxes (decorative lines and frames), and Picture Boxes (.BMP or .WMF picture files). You drag these boxes around and resize them until you have the look you want, and then print. It's not all that difficult.

But you do have to understand that the various types of boxes are treated as objects and that each type has its own rank in the ViaPrint hierarchy. For example, Line Boxes have the lowest priority—all other objects are placed on top of Line Boxes. Next are Angle Boxes, then Text Boxes, and finally Picture Boxes. So to get at a Line Box that is covered by a Text Box, you'll need to move the Text Box so that the Line Box is visible.

TIP

Because ViaPrint can look so complicated, you might want to open one of the examples included with the program (File ➤ Open Label Design) and play around with it for a while before trying something more complex.

Double-click on the ViaPrint icon to open the main screen, shown in Figure 13.1. Select Page ➤ Label Size and Page Setup. This will open a window like the one shown in Figure 13.2, where you can select from 30 preset Avery label sizes or specify your own custom settings. Click on the Okay button when you're done.

text boxes

As you can see in Figure 13.1, there's a single Text Box that says Blank Line, highlighted by resizing tabs. The tabs will appear red on a color monitor. To change the size of a Text Box, click on the left or right resizing tab (the mouse pointer will change to a double-headed arrow when it's in the correct position) and hold down the left mouse button while you drag the box to a new size.

■ **FIGURE 13.1**
ViaPrint's opening screen

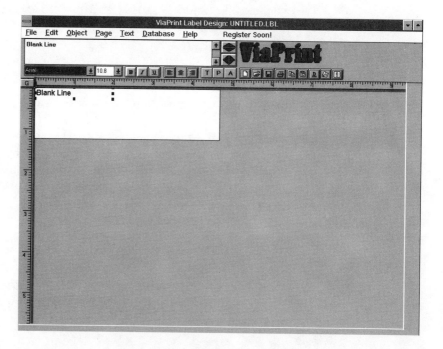

■ **FIGURE 13.2**
Choose the label
size you want to
use or make your
own custom
settings.

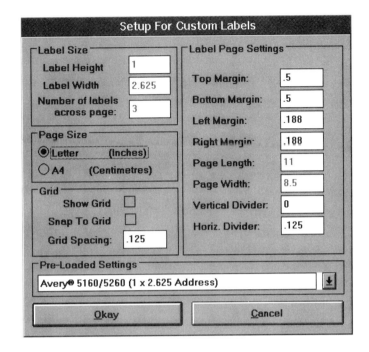

As you enter text, it will be displayed in the current Text Box (and simultaneously on the label) with the text wrapping to fit the box width and the box expanding in height as you type.

You can move the Text Box to any position on the label by placing the mouse pointer on the Text Box. (The pointer will change from a cross hair to an up arrow when it's positioned over a moveable object.) Click on the Text Box and drag it to the new location. Indicators on the horizontal and vertical rulers will help you line up Text Boxes. Select Snap To Grid in the page setup window (see Figure 13.2) and the Text Box will align itself to the current grid setting.

Above the label, you can use the font name, font size, and font style option (bold, italic, and underline) tools to display the text in your Text Box the way you want it. You can also align the text in your Text

Box by selecting the left justification, centered text, or right justification buttons:

To add another Text Box, select Add Text Box from the Object menu.

picture boxes

To add a picture to your label, select Object ➤ Add Picture Box. From the File Type list box in the File window, choose either .BMP or .WMF (Windows MetaFile). Then select the picture file you want to display and click on the OK button.

To resize a picture, move the pointer over the resizing tab that corresponds to the direction you want to stretch or shrink the Picture Box. When the mouse pointer is over the resizing tab, the pointer will change to a double arrow. Press the left mouse button and hold it down while dragging the corner or edge of the Picture Box until it's the size you want.

TIP

Got a .GIF or a .TIF file you'd like to use? Photolab (Chapter 8) can convert the picture file to .BMP format and then you can add it to any ViaPrint label.

line boxes

To create a Line Box, first you need to draw the size and position for it on your label. Move the mouse cursor to the point where you want the upper left corner of the Line Box to be. The mouse cursor *must* be in the shape of a cross hair—if it's not, then you're already on top of another Line Box, Text Box, Angle Box, or Picture Box.

Click the left mouse button and, holding it down, drag the mouse cursor down and to the right. As you do this, a box outline will appear on the label. When this box is the approximate size of the Line Box you want to create, release the mouse button.

Select Object ➤ Draw Line Box and your Line Box will be created and highlighted—ready to reposition and resize as you wish.

To fill the Line Box with color, select the Line Box and then select Object ➤ Object Color. If you choose a color other than white, the box appears opaque—you can't see through it. If you choose white, the Line Box is transparent.

angle boxes

Angle Boxes can display text at an angle. They work a lot like Text Boxes, with the following exceptions:

- ❑ Because they can rotate, Angle Boxes are as high as they are wide. This makes them a little awkward because they cover any Line Boxes they're over. For this reason, it's usually a good idea to add Angle Boxes after other objects have been created and placed on the label.

- ❑ Angle Boxes print only in black.

- ❑ When an Angle Box is currently selected, a rotate control in the form of a slider bar will appear in the upper right corner on your screen. Use this control to change the angle at which your text is displayed.

Not all fonts can be rotated, though most TrueType fonts are okay. Printout results for Angle Boxes are not always accurate! Test first by printing a sample on scrap paper.

To add another Angle Box, select Add Angle Box from the Object menu. Figure 13.3 shows a sample label with a Picture Box, a Text Box, and an Angle Box.

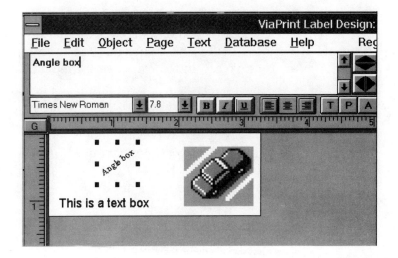

Experiment with different looks and approaches. It won't be long before you'll be churning out snappy-looking labels in minutes.

TIP
ViaPrint will also print labels from a database. Select Database ➤ Use Database. If you need help, double-click on the ViaPrint Documentation icon in the ViaPrint group for specific instructions.

▪ ▪ ▪ ▪ ▪ ▪ ▪ ▪ ▪ ▪ contacting the programmer

ViaPrint version 2.0 is copyrighted 1994 by Casey Butler. Casey really tries to make it worth your while to register. If you send him $29.50, he'll send you the registered version of ViaPrint, which has additional capabilities. You'll also get technical support, a printed manual, more shareware, and a free registered copy of his popular arcade game, *Heavy Water Jogger*. To register, send a check for $29.50 to:

Viable Software Alternatives
P.O. Box 98134
Las Vegas, NV 89193-8134

To use your MasterCard or Visa, call 800-854-4902 (this number is only for orders). An address and phone number to register in Europe is in the VIAPRINT.WRI file (search for "The Thompson Partnership").

For technical support, questions about orders, site licensing information, and the like, call 618-549-5227. Or you can send Casey a message on CompuServe, where his address is 72043,46.

P A R T . . . .

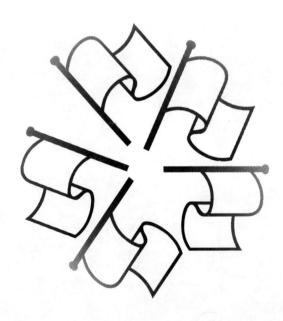

5

Desktop Accessories

What are those dumb fashion magazines always telling you to do? Accessorize!

So here are some desktop accessories to help you automate tasks that ordinarily take a lot of time and effort. They'll help you compress and decompress files, use DOS commands without leaving Windows, and put sticky notes on your desktop or attach them to your documents whenever you please. I consider these programs to be among the cream of the shareware utilities.

Program 14

WinZip

Perhaps you're one of those lucky souls with a multi-gigabyte hard disk so you *never* need to compress files to save space. But even under those fortunate circumstances, you'll still need a *decompressing* program for files you download from bulletin boards or files you receive from clients and friends. Most file compression programs work only in DOS, so you usually have to exit to DOS to get the job done. WinZip puts an end to all that nonsense.

With WinZip you can compress and decompress files without ever leaving Windows. WinZip supports drag-and-drop and a host of other features. If you have an anti-virus program on your system, WinZip will search for it and then, if you wish, run any archived file through the anti-virus strainer and catch any bad bugs before they find their way into your system.

▪ installing

To install WinZip, follow these steps:

1. Put Disk 2 in drive A. Open File Manager and click on the A drive icon.

2. Highlight the file WZIP.EXE and then select File ➤ Copy from the File Manager menu. Copy the file to a temporary location on your hard disk.

3. Go to the directory where you've placed WZIP.EXE and double-click on the file name. The files inside WZIP.EXE will be extracted.

 TIP

If the files don't show up in the File Manager window after you extract them, press F5 to refresh the view. F5 also refreshes the drive window in Norton Desktop for Windows.

4. Double-click on the file INSTALL.EXE. If you *don't* want the program to have its own group inside Program Manager, click on the Add Icons to Program Manager box to remove the check mark. When that box is clear, the program will still be installed in its own directory, but you'll have to run it by double-clicking on the .EXE program from a File Manager window.

5. If you want the program to be in your StartUp group, make sure that box is checked. Then click on OK.

6. If the INSTALL program finds duplicate files on your hard disk (this sometimes happens, particularly with .DLL files), it'll let you know. If the INSTALL version of the file is newer (check the date) or larger, then let it overwrite the older file.

After installation is complete, delete all the files from the temporary location. These files aren't necessary to run the program and just take up hard disk space.

TIP
WinZip is a very handy program to have percolating on your desktop when you need it, so you may want to put it in the StartUp group. If you decide to do that, enable the Run Minimized option in the Properties dialog box after you install WinZip. The program will run as an icon at the bottom of your screen.

understanding archives

If you've already used PKZIP and PKUNZIP or other archiving programs, you are excused from reading this section and should go right on to "Getting Started."

Archives are just files that contain other files. Some files—particularly text files and graphic files—are quite large considering the amount of real information they hold. Archiving programs *compress* the file by taking out the extraneous information, thereby reducing the size of the file by as much as 90 percent. When you want the file back, you just run the archive through a *decompressing* program and presto! The file's back to its normal size. The terms "archived file," "compressed file," and "zipped file" are pretty much interchangeable.

Archives usually have file names ending with .ZIP (by far the most common extension), .ARC, .LZH, or .ARJ, depending on which archiving program created them. However, if you have WinZip, it won't matter to you because WinZip handles all these formats transparently.

getting started

WinZip has lots of bells and whistles for compression and decompression options. Most of the time, though, you'll just do simple operations such as extracting files from an archive and making up a new archive out of files you choose.

decompressing an archived file

When you get a compressed file, you may want to do one or all of the following:

- See what files are inside.
- Examine the contents of one of the files inside.
- Extract certain files from inside the archive, but not the entire archive.
- Extract all the files inside.

With WinZip you can easily do all these things (and more). The easiest method is to highlight the file name in File Manager and drag the file to WinZip (which you have cleverly placed, minimized, on your desktop). Or you can double-click on the WinZip icon in the WinZip group and then use File ➤ Open Archive to load the file you want to examine. Either way you'll end up with a window that looks something like Figure 14.1.

To extract all the files in the archive, just click on the Extract button. WinZip prompts you to give a location for the files and then extracts them for you.

To extract just one file, highlight it and click on the Extract button. To view the contents of one of the files, highlight it and click on View.

Now here's the "more" I mentioned earlier—namely the CheckOut feature that's activated when you click on the button by that name. CheckOut creates a Program Manager group containing one icon for each file in the archive. If a particular file is executable, double-clicking on the icon runs the program. If the file has an association in Windows, double-clicking on the icon will load the file in the associated program. Otherwise, double-clicking on the icon loads the

◻ **FIGURE 14.1**
WinZip with an
archived file

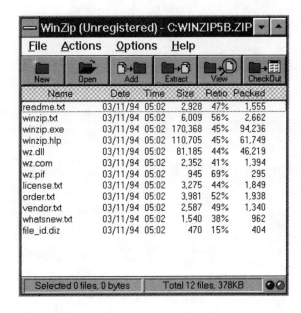

file in the WinZip Default Association program (specified in the Program Locations dialog box). When you're done poking around, you can close the archive and WinZip will prompt you to keep the newly made Program Manager group or delete it.

making a new archive file

To compress one or more files into a new archive, you can either click on the New button and navigate your way through the dialog boxes or just drag-and-drop files into WinZip.

Either way you'll be prompted for a file name for the new archive. The Add files dialog box is shown in Figure 14.2. If you don't specify an extension, WinZip uses the .ZIP extension by default; see the "Settings and Options" section for more on setting your preferences.

The default settings are optimal for most purposes, but if you're ever really cramped for space, you might want to choose Maximum in the Compression drop-down list to squeeze your files into the minimum possible space.

■ FIGURE 14.2
The Add files dialog box works like other Windows boxes. You can use the Ctrl and Shift keys with the mouse to select multiple files.

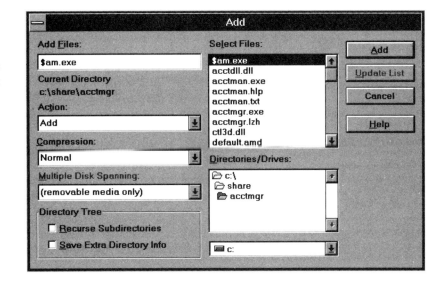

After your files are all added, just c⸝ ⸝ose Close Archive from the File menu and you're done.

■ ■ ■ ■ ■ ■ ■ ■ ■ ■ ■ ■ ■ settings and options

The Options ➤ Configuration dialog box lets you specify many details about WinZip. For example, once you get comfortable with WinZip, you may want to get rid of some of the options under Prompt. This is also where you can change the default archiving method that WinZip uses.

The rest of the settings (except for those that are obviously cosmetic, like Use Large Toolbar Buttons) should be left alone until you've had a chance to work with WinZip for a while. Then you can go spelunking in the documentation should you so desire, and fiddle with the settings as much as you like. However, WinZip will work splendidly without any changes whatsoever.

TIP

Under the Actions menu, there's an option called Make .EXE File. This option will turn any file into a self-extracting archive. This won't work for the .ZIP format unless you already have the full PKZIP program from PKWARE, Inc., and WinZip knows where to find it (see Options ➤ Program Locations).

▪ ▪ ▪ ▪ ▪ ▪ ▪ ▪ ▪ contacting the programmer

WinZip version 5.0b is copyrighted 1991-1993 by Nico Mak Computing, Inc. You're authorized to use this shareware version for 21 days and then you're obliged to register it. Nico's excellent work can be registered for $29 for a single copy. (He also offers site licenses for multiple copies. Prices for those are on the order form.)

Send a check for $29 to:

> Nico Mak Computing, Inc.
> P.O. Box 919
> Bristol, CT 06011-0919

Credit card orders can be placed with the Public Software Library at 1-800-242-4PSL, by fax at 713-524-6398, or by sending CompuServe email to 71355,470. These PSL numbers are for orders only. Any questions about the status of a shipment, registration options, product details, technical support, and all that sort of stuff should be directed to Nico Mak at the address above or at the following email addresses:

> CompuServe: 70056,241
> BIX: Nico_Mak

Program 15

The SmilerShell

One of the reasons we're all living in Windows these days is because so many things are easier in Windows than they are in DOS. The graphical interface, pull-down menus, and all that stuff is easy to learn and transferable from one program to another. However, there are still those occasions when you need or want to use the DOS command line. The SmilerShell gives you that DOS command line without your ever having to leave Windows. The program is graphical, it has menus, and it's generally a painless way to run all the usual internal DOS commands quickly and seamlessly.

▪   **installing**

To install SmilerShell, just follow these steps:

1. Put Disk 2 in drive A. Open File Manager and click on the A drive icon.

2. Highlight the file SMILER.EXE and then select File ➤ Copy from the File Manager menu. Copy the file to a temporary location on your hard disk.

3. Go to the directory where you've placed SMILER.EXE and double-click on the file name.

4. Read the information on the screen (or ignore it) and press Y to continue. Next double-click on the INSTALL.EXE file and the program will install itself. By default, the program will make a Program Manager group for itself as well as install itself in the StartUp group. This is a good arrangement, because you'll want SmilerShell right at hand when you need it.

5. If the INSTALL program finds duplicate files on your hard disk (this sometimes happens, particularly with .DLL files), it'll let you know. If the INSTALL version of the file is newer (check the date) or larger, go ahead and let it overwrite the older file.

After installation is complete, delete all the files from the temporary location. These files aren't necessary to run the program and just take up hard disk space.

TIP

If the files don't show up in the File Manager window after you extract them, press F5 to refresh the view. F5 also refreshes the drive window in Norton Desktop for Windows.

getting started

The first time you run SmilerShell, the program very politely asks for permission to make an .INI file for you. Actually, there's no reasonable way to say no, so just let the program proceed. The .INI file can always be changed later, should you need to do so.

When you double-click on the SmilerShell icon, you have everything you need to run any DOS command. Just type the command in the box:

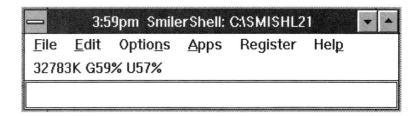

But SmilerShell is in many ways much better than a boring old DOS prompt. The following sections describe some of its features.

the apps menu

The Apps menu lets you quickly load your favorite applications. Click on Notepad Autoexec to get an idea of how it works. The Windows Notepad program is opened with your AUTOEXEC.BAT file loaded. Select Edit Apps List to add more programs or to change the ones already on the menu.

command stack

Every time you run a command, it's saved in the command stack. To find a previous command, type the first letter or two of the command and then press the ↑ or ↓ key. ↑ searches back and ↓ searches forward, although it doesn't really matter which direction you go because it's a circular file and eventually you'll get back to where you started. To see a full command history, select File ➤ List Commands.

file associations

SmilerShell recognizes all the file associations set up in Windows. Just type a file name and SmilerShell finds the program associated with the file and runs it. So if you type in *filename*.CAL, SmilerShell will run the Windows Calendar program with *filename*.CAL loaded. Type in *filename*.WRI and the Windows Write program is started with the specified file loaded and ready.

smart directory changes

Do a quick directory change by typing DC followed by the first few letters of the directory you want to be in. If there's more than one choice based on the letters you've entered, SmilerShell will open a list box of the possible matching files so you can pick which one you want.

toggle dos in a window or full-screen

By default, the DOS in Window option is set to On. If you want to run something full-screen, just precede the command with a greater-than sign (>). Similarly, if you set the option so that your commands run the other way (full-screen), you can make a command run in a window by typing > first.

In addition, you can tinker with the settings in the Options menu or make more permanent changes in the .INI file.

TIP

If, through an attack of blissful ignorance, you happen to mess up the SMISHELL.INI file in some irrevocable way, don't worry about it. Just delete it. The next time you start SmilerShell, the program will build you a brand new .INI file.

putting the shell in its place

You can set up SmilerShell in a number of different ways. The best setups are as follows:

- Open the Options menu and make sure there's a check next to Topmost and Clock but *not* one in front of Menu. Use the mouse to make the SmilerShell window as small as possible and then drag the whole thing to a corner of your screen. The clock is still visible, as is enough of the command line area so that you can type in a command. The window will look like this:

  To get the menus back, open the Control Box menu in the upper left corner and click on Show SmilerShell menu.

- To make the window smaller, remove the check from Options ➤ Titlebar and you'll get a window that's even tinier:

  To move the window once it no longer has a titlebar, you need to place the mouse pointer inside the command line area and click on the right mouse button. You can drag the window to a new location as long as you hold the mouse button down. Press Alt+M to toggle the menu back on.

◘ For another approach, open the Options menu and toggle the Topmost setting on. Then click on the maximize button. This will put SmilerShell at the very top of your screen, where it'll occupy only a narrow band of space.

◘ ◘ ◘ ◘ ◘ ◘ ◘ ◘ ◘ contacting the programmer

SmilerShell version 2.1 is copyrighted 1994 by Barry Smiler. If you like the program and want to keep it on your system, registration is a mere $19.95. There's also a version called SmilerShell Pro that costs $29.95 (for a preview of the Pro version, see the SmilerShell Pro demo icon in the SmilerShell group window).

Register and, in addition to the usual disk and manual, you'll get two more free utilities, a bunch of discount offers, a free Compu-Serve startup kit, and additional shareware. Pretty impressive!

To register, send $19.95 (for SmilerShell) or $29.95 (for SmilerShell Pro) plus $3.50 for shipping to:

Barry Smiler
Bardon Data Systems
1023 Key Route Blvd.
Albany, CA 94706

To pay with a MasterCard or Visa (and get instant relief from those reminder screens), call 510-526-8470. You can also order by calling 1-800-242-4775 (weekdays 7 a.m.–6 p.m. Central Time), though you won't get your registration number on the spot.

Read the REGISTER.TXT file for information on registering in Australia, Canada, England, France, Japan—and who knows where else!

For technical support, questions, and suggestions for the next version, contact Barry at the above address or send email to him on CompuServe: 72340,375.

Program 16

WinPost

Ever get so absorbed in your work that you forget to call back a client? Remember you have to go to the bank only after it's closed? Or leave your kids waiting outside the school until the principal calls?

Well, before you get yelled at *again*, install WinPost, handy little notes that pop up and remind you about tasks and deadlines you might otherwise forget. The notes can be hidden until you want to see them and configured in a variety of ways to suit your needs.

In addition to their reminder function, WinPost notes can be attached to any OLE-compliant document (in other words, documents made by Word for Windows, Excel, or any other program that supports OLE) just as the paper version of sticky notes are attached to paper documents.

■ **installing**

To install WinPost, follow these steps:

1. Put Disk 2 in drive A. Open File Manager and click on the A drive icon.

2. Highlight the file WPOST.EXE and then select File ➤ Copy from the File Manager menu. Copy the file to a temporary location on your hard disk.

3. Go to the directory where you've placed WPOST.EXE and double-click on the file name. The files inside WPOST.EXE will be extracted.

TIP

If the files don't show up in the File Manager window after you extract them, press F5 to refresh the view. F5 also refreshes the drive window in Norton Desktop for Windows.

4. Double-click on the file SETUP.EXE. By default, the installation program will put WinPost in its own program group. After installation is complete, you may want to put WinPost in your StartUp group, too, so it'll always be ready on your desktop when you need it.

After installation is complete, delete all the files from the temporary location. These files aren't necessary to run the program and just take up hard disk space.

■ ■ ■ ■ ■ ■ ■ ■ ■ ■ ■ ■ ■ ■ ■ ■ ■ **getting started**

WinPost will appear as an icon at the bottom of your screen if you installed it in your StartUp group. Otherwise, you'll need to go to the WinPost group and double-click on the WinPost icon. In either case, when you click once on the icon at the bottom of the screen, you'll get the full WinPost menu shown in Figure 16.1.

◘ FIGURE 16.1
The full WinPost
main menu

◘ FIGURE 16.1
The full WinPost
main menu

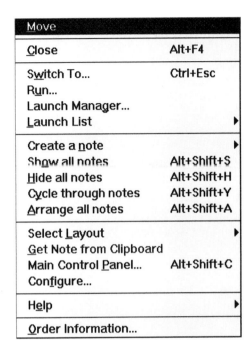

Choose Create a note (and the size of the note you want) to get started. This will open the note-sized box shown in Figure 16.2.

Type in the message you want on your note. When you're finished, click on the control box in the upper left corner to get the menu shown in Figure 16.3. You can hide the note, insert the day and time, and so forth from this menu.

◘ FIGURE 16.2
A WinPost note

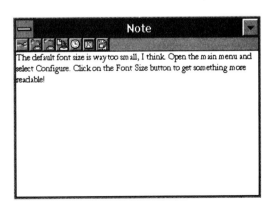

■ **FIGURE 16.3**
The menu that
opens from a note's
control box

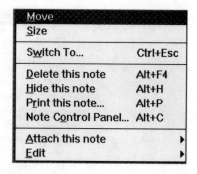

Move	
Size	
Switch To...	Ctrl+Esc
Delete this note	Alt+F4
Hide this note	Alt+H
Print this note...	Alt+P
Note Control Panel...	Alt+C
Attach this note	▶
Edit	▶

The itsy-bitsy, teeny-weeny toolbar on each note has icons for the following functions (reading from left to right): Cut, Copy, Paste, Copy note contents to Clipboard, Insert date/time stamp, Display note control panel, and Attach note (including the title bar) to Clipboard.

To set an alarm, click on the Note Control Panel button. In this panel, shown in Figure 16.4, you can choose a color for the note and select other settings as well. Select the Alarm On box and set the time for the alarm to wake…er, *notify* you. You can choose the sound effect you want for the alarm, or you can choose silence.

TIP

You won't get any sound at all unless you have system sounds enabled. To do that, go to the Control Panel (in the Main group of Windows) and select Sounds. Put a check in the box marked "Enable System Sounds" and then click on OK.

To make settings for all your notes, choose Configure from the WinPost main menu (shown in Figure 16.1). Here you can choose the default color, size, and font for all your notes.

There are also provisions under Configure for setting up hot keys— one set to bring the WinPost icon to the forefront and another to automatically open up a new note.

Select Main Control Panel from the main WinPost menu to search your notes for any word or phrase. You can also print your notes or even save them to disk.

■ FIGURE 16.4
Here you can set
the alarm and an
individual note's
color and title.

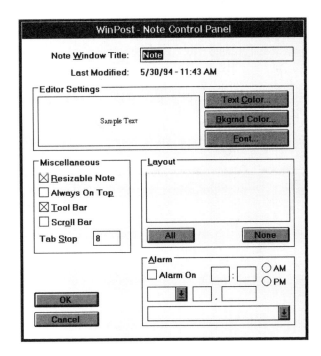

■ FIGURE 16.4
Here you can set
the alarm and an
individual note's
color and title.

⬛ ⬛ ⬛ ⬛ ⬛ using notes with an ole document

OLE, which stands for Object Linking and Embedding, is a protocol for compound documents. It allows data from one application to be embedded within another application's data. WinPost makes use of this protocol to allow the user to "attach" a note to any OLE-compliant document, much like you would a yellow sticky note. Once embedded, the note becomes a part of the document; thus, the document can be moved to another system, and the note can still be viewed and edited as long as WinPost is running on the system.

attaching a note

To attach a note, follow these steps:

1. Type the note. Choose Attach this note from the control box menu (see Figure 16.3). In the submenu, choose

either Cut to Clipboard or Copy to Clipboard. Or you can click on the Attach Note button on the icon toolbar (the last button on the right).

2. Switch to the target document. Place the cursor in the position where you want the note to be.

3. Choose Edit ➤ Paste Special. This will embed the note into the document at the cursor position.

editing an attached note

To edit an attached note, double-click on the note in the document. This will open up the note in a separate window. Make your edits and then close the note window.

contacting the programmer

WinPost version 3.2b is copyrighted 1990-1993 by Eastern Mountain Software, Inc. The programmer is the very talented Nobuya "Higgy" Higashiyama. You can register the program for $30 (U.S.) in Canada, the U.S., or Mexico. The fee goes up to $35 for other countries. Information on site licenses is included under Order Information in the main menu. To register, send your check to:

Eastern Mountain Software
P.O. Box 20178
Columbus, OH 43220
Voice: 614-798-0910

To register using a credit card, call 1-800-242-4PSL or fax an order to 713-524-6398. The part number for WinPost 3.2b is 10302. These numbers are for ordering only. For questions about the program, contact Higgy at the Columbus address and phone number above.

Program 17

D'Menu

Lots of programs come with functions attached to the right mouse button, but if you've ever wished for a menu you could configure yourself, D'Menu is the package that will do it for you. Assign programs, functions, and files *within* programs to the menu and you can zip around your computer like Mario Andretti on a very good day.

NOTE

The only drawback to D'Menu that I've found is that it doesn't work with Norton Desktop for Windows version 3.0. There may be other programs that don't like it, but it probably won't do any harm to try it out. If it doesn't work for you in some important area, just delete it from your system and appreciate the sixteen other really useful programs you got!

- - - - - - - - - - - - - - - - - - - # installing

To install D'Menu, follow these steps:

1. Put Disk 1 in drive A. Open File Manager and click on the A drive icon.

2. Highlight the file DMENU.EXE and then select File ➤ Copy from the File Manager menu. Copy the file to a temporary location on your hard disk.

3. Go to the directory where you've placed DMENU.EXE and double-click on the file name. The files inside DMENU.EXE will be extracted.

TIP

If the files don't show up in the File Manager window after you extract them, press F5 to refresh the view.

4. Double-click on the file INSTALL.EXE. By default, the installation program will put D'Menu in its own program group and in your StartUp group.

5. If the INSTALL program finds duplicate files on your hard disk (this sometimes happens, particularly with .DLL files), it'll let you know. If the INSTALL version of the file is newer (check the date) or larger, go ahead and let it overwrite the older file.

After installation is complete, delete all the files from the temporary location. These files aren't necessary to run the program and just take up hard disk space.

- - - - - - - - - - - - - - - - # getting started

After installing D'Menu, all you have to do to get it running is double-click on the D'Menu icon. Move your mouse pointer to a blank spot on the desktop and then click once with the right mouse button to get the starter menu:

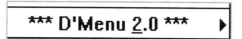

Click on the ➤ on the right side and select Setup. This will open the Setup window shown in Figure 17.1. This window just shows what's currently on the menu—namely, nothing. To add something to the menu, click on the Add button.

The Add window, shown in Figure 17.2, is where you configure the menu. Everything works according to the usual Windows standards. In the first line, Menu Text, you supply the description as you want it to show on the menu. In the second line, provide the file name and the path of the program you want to execute when this menu item is selected (use the Browse button if you're not sure about the exact name or location). You can type in the working directory, if applicable.

◻ **FIGURE 17.1**
The Setup window when you first open it

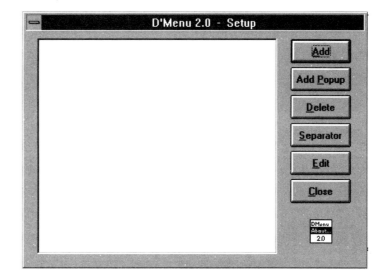

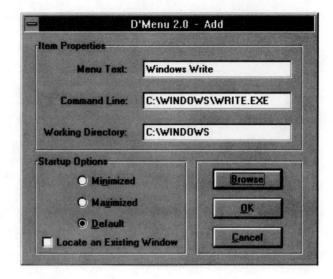

TIP

A very nice feature is the Locate an Existing Window check box. If this box is checked, D'Menu will look to see if the program is already open. If it is, it'll bring that window to the foreground. If the box is not checked, D'Menu will launch a new instance of the program without checking to see if it's already open somewhere on the desktop.

You can keep adding items to your menu in this way, up to a maximum of 99 (though that does seem just a little excessive). To divide menu items into groups, click on the Separator button to add a line of dashes. Click on the Close button when you're done.

popup items

The so-called "popup" items are a way of making what I'd call cascaded menus. In other words, you can have a main item on the menu that will open up a submenu. This will help you keep the main menu to a manageable length.

The main listing is the popup, and the cascaded items are attached to it. Here's how to make a popup:

1. Open the Setup window and click on the Add Popup button.

2. Type in the name for the main listing as you want it to appear on the menu, and then click on OK.

3. Click on Add. Confirm that you want to add the new items to the popup.

4. In the new window, provide all the usual information about the program and its whereabouts. Click on the OK button when you're done.

Figure 17.3 shows a Setup window where I've made a main menu item called Windows Utilities with Calendar, Windows Write, and Control Panel cascaded under that entry. The final result, as it appears in the menu, is shown in Figure 17.4. When I click on Windows Utilities, the submenu opens.

□ **FIGURE 17.3**
Making a popup list of Windows Utilities

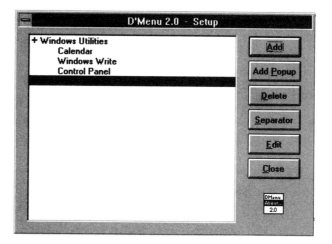

Windows Utilities	Calendar
*** D'Menu 2.0 ***	Windows Write
	Control Panel

TIP
You can use D'Menu to make a quick exit from Windows, too. Just click on the ➤ next to the D'Menu name and select Exit Windows.

contacting the programmer

D'Menu version 2.0 is copyrighted 1993 by David S. Reinhart Associates. For the very modest fee of $15, you can register the program, get the next upgrade free, and get rid of the reminder-to-register screens. Send a check or money order to:

David S. Reinhart Associates
1004 Marticville Rd.
Pequea, PA 17565

Voice: 717-284-3736
CompuServe: 71572,304

MAKE A GOOD COMPUTER EVEN BETTER.

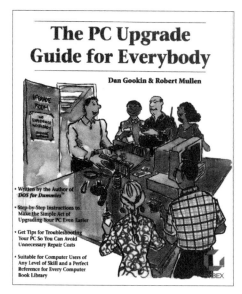

The PC Upgrade Guide for Everybody

Dan Gookin & Robert Mullen

- Written by the Author of *DOS for Dummies*
- Step-by-Step Instructions to Make the Simple Act of Upgrading Your PC Even Easier
- Get Tips for Troubleshooting Your PC So You Can Avoid Unnecessary Repair Costs
- Suitable for Computer Users of Any Level of Skill and a Perfect Reference for Every Computer Book Library

350pp. ISBN: 1301-X.

The *PC Upgrade Guide for Everybody* is the no-hassle, do-it-yourself PC upgrade guide for everyone. If you know the difference between a screwdriver and a pair of pliers, this book is for you.

Inside you'll find step-by-step instructions for installing hardware to make your computer even more fun and productive. Add memory chips, CD-ROM drives and more to your PC.

You'll also learn how to diagnose minor PC problems and decide whether to repair or replace faulty components —without schlepping your PC to the shop and paying big bucks.

SYBEX. Help Yourself.

2021 Challenger Drive
Alameda, CA 94501
1-800-227-2346

SYBEX

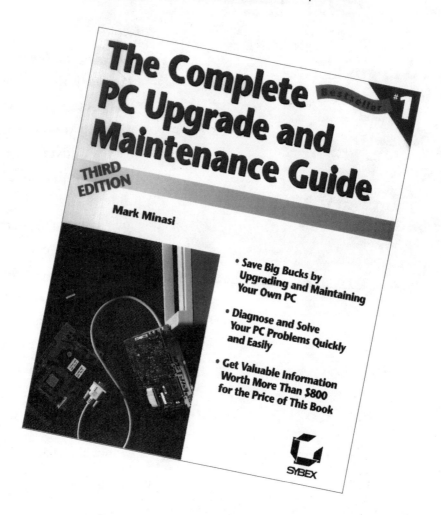

Go from zero to 60 on the Information Superhighway— in a flash!

What's a good modem? Isn't there some *simple* explanation of the "Internet?" How is it different from Prodigy or CompuServe? What's the cost?

At last, here's *the* book on joining the online community, from SYBEX.

Now available wherever computer books are sold.

274 pages.
ISBN 1417-2

SYBEX

Shortcuts to Understanding.

SYBEX, Inc.
2021 Challenger Drive
Alameda, CA 94501
1-800-227-2346
1-510-523-8233

All the facts
about WinFax.

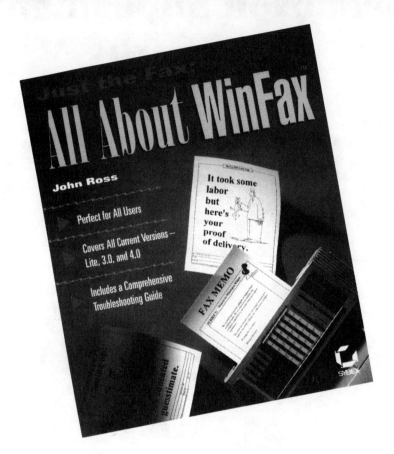

Whether you got WinFax Lite free with your modem, or just
went out and bought WinFax Pro 3.0 or 4.0, you'll appreciate
the frank, troubleshooting approach of this companion for the
popular Windows computer fax software.

*Now available
wherever computer
books are sold.*

376 pages.
ISBN 1462-8

SYBEX

Shortcuts to Understanding.

SYBEX, Inc.
2021 Challenger Drive
Alameda, CA 94501
1-800-227-2346
1-510-523-8233

⌂ The Rest of the Best of Home Office Shareware ⌂

I hope you find the seventeen enclosed *Home Office ShareWarehouse* programs interesting and useful. It wasn't easy deciding which programs to include. There's a lot of terrific shareware out there, but only seventeen programs would fit on the two disks included with this book.

That's why I put together this special offer for readers of *The Home Office ShareWarehouse*. You can get **two more disks** jam-packed with great shareware for the home office—more selections from the cream of the shareware crop. And as a special bonus I collected all three runtime files required by Visual Basic programs. These are sometimes difficult to find, but you can get them **FREE** with your order.

Sharon Crawford

	ITEM	Quantity	Price	Subtotal
DISK SET:	**More Windows Home Office Shareware** Two high-density 3½" disks full of useful business utilities, programs, and other cool stuff.		$15.95	
BONUS:	**All Three Visual Basic Runtime Files** One of these three files is required by every program developed with Microsoft's Visual Basic. With this disk you'll have the correct version for any Visual Basic program you want to run. FREE with your order.		FREE	FREE
	Shipping and handling ($4 USA and Canada, $9 elsewhere)			$
	California residents please add 8.5% sales tax			$
	TOTAL			$

☐ **YES, send me the DISK SET and BONUS as indicated above**

☐ I have enclosed a check or money order in U.S. funds.

☐ Bill me.   [ ] MasterCard

[ ] Visa   *card number:* _____   *expiration date:* ___ / ___

Name: _____

Address: _____

_____

_____

Phone: _____   Electronic mail: _____

Send this form (or make a copy or write a note if you don't want to rip out this page) to:

Home Office Shareware
Bardon Data Systems
1023 Key Route Blvd.
Albany, CA 94706-2321
Orders only call (800) 242-4775

We generally ship within 24 hours, but to be on the safe side allow up to 4 weeks for delivery.

GET A FREE CATALOG JUST FOR EXPRESSING YOUR OPINION.

Help us improve our books and get a *FREE* full-color catalog in the bargain. Please complete this form, pull out this page and send it in today. The address is on the reverse side.

Name _____   Company _____

Address _____   City _____ State ____ Zip _____

Phone (___) _____

1. **How would you rate the overall quality of this book?**

   ❑ Excellent
   ❑ Very Good
   ❑ Good
   ❑ Fair
   ❑ Below Average
   ❑ Poor

2. **What were the things you liked most about the book? (Check all that apply)**

   ❑ Pace
   ❑ Format
   ❑ Writing Style
   ❑ Examples
   ❑ Table of Contents
   ❑ Index
   ❑ Price
   ❑ Illustrations
   ❑ Type Style
   ❑ Cover
   ❑ Depth of Coverage
   ❑ Fast Track Notes

3. **What were the things you liked *least* about the book? (Check all that apply)**

   ❑ Pace
   ❑ Format
   ❑ Writing Style
   ❑ Examples
   ❑ Table of Contents
   ❑ Index
   ❑ Price
   ❑ Illustrations
   ❑ Type Style
   ❑ Cover
   ❑ Depth of Coverage
   ❑ Fast Track Notes

4. **Where did you buy this book?**

   ❑ Bookstore chain
   ❑ Small independent bookstore
   ❑ Computer store
   ❑ Wholesale club
   ❑ College bookstore
   ❑ Technical bookstore
   ❑ Other _____

5. **How did you decide to buy this particular book?**

   ❑ Recommended by friend
   ❑ Recommended by store personnel
   ❑ Author's reputation
   ❑ Sybex's reputation
   ❑ Read book review in _____
   ❑ Other _____

6. **How did you pay for this book?**

   ❑ Used own funds
   ❑ Reimbursed by company
   ❑ Received book as a gift

7. **What is your level of experience with the subject covered in this book?**

   ❑ Beginner
   ❑ Intermediate
   ❑ Advanced

8. **How long have you been using a computer?**

   years _____

   months _____

9. **Where do you most often use your computer?**

   ❑ Home
   ❑ Work

   ❑ Both
   ❑ Other _____

10. **What kind of computer equipment do you have? (Check all that apply)**

    ❑ PC Compatible Desktop Computer
    ❑ PC Compatible Laptop Computer
    ❑ Apple/Mac Computer
    ❑ Apple/Mac Laptop Computer
    ❑ CD ROM
    ❑ Fax Modem
    ❑ Data Modem
    ❑ Scanner
    ❑ Sound Card
    ❑ Other _____

11. **What other kinds of software packages do you ordinarily use?**

    ❑ Accounting
    ❑ Databases
    ❑ Networks
    ❑ Apple/Mac
    ❑ Desktop Publishing
    ❑ Spreadsheets
    ❑ CAD
    ❑ Games
    ❑ Word Processing
    ❑ Communications
    ❑ Money Management
    ❑ Other _____

12. **What operating systems do you ordinarily use?**

    ❑ DOS
    ❑ OS/2
    ❑ Windows
    ❑ Apple/Mac
    ❑ Windows NT
    ❑ Other _____

13. On what computer-related subject(s) would you like to see more books?

_____

_____

_____

_____

14. Do you have any other comments about this book? (Please feel free to use a separate piece of paper if you need more room)

_____

_____

_____

_____

– – – – – – – – – – – – – – PLEASE FOLD, SEAL, AND MAIL TO SYBEX – – – – – – – – – – – – –

SYBEX INC.
Department M
2021 Challenger Drive
Alameda, CA
94501

About the Disks

The Home Office ShareWarehouse includes two high-density 3½″ floppy disks containing the various shareware programs discussed in the book. A high-density disk drive is required to download the programs from the disks.

What's on the Disks? Disk 1 contains Above & Beyond (ABEYOND.EXE), an excellent Personal Information Manager; Account Manager (ACCTMGR.EXE), which helps you keep track of multiple clients; Business Cards (BUSCARDS.EXE), which organizes your thoughts and ideas so you can retrieve them easily; Practical PhoneBook (PHONEBK.EXE), which allows you to dial clients with the click of a mouse; Chartist (CHARTS.EXE), which helps you make beautiful and practical charts; FontLine (FNTLINE.EXE), which converts text into bitmaps; Grammar Expert (GRAMEXP.EXE), which provides on-line grammar help without the annoyances of most grammar checkers; and D'Menu (DMENU.EXE), which turns your right mouse button into a customized menu. Some of the shareware programs included in this book require another program called Visual Basic Runtime (VBRUN3.EXE) in order for them to load properly, so Disk 1 includes this program as well.

Disk 2 contains Task Planner (TASKPLAN.EXE), an affordable task scheduler; PageMate (PAGEMATE.EXE), which pages you when your answering machine takes a call; Photolab (PHOTO.EXE), which puts command of computer graphics at your fingertips; FontSpec Pro (FONTSPEC.EXE), which helps you organize your fonts into manageable groups; PostMaster (POST.EXE), which prints envelopes without a word processor; ViaPrint (VPRINT.EXE), which helps you print labels, flyers, and business cards with ease; WinZip (WZIP.EXE), which allows you to compress and decompress files (or parts of a file) within Windows; SmilerShell (SMILER.EXE), which allows you to run DOS commands within Windows; and WinPost (WPOST.EXE), which sets up electronic sticky notes so you can remind yourself about things you need to do.

What Is Shareware? For an explanation of how shareware works, see the section called "What Is Shareware" in the Introduction.

What about Installation? Some programs load differently from others, so directions for installing each program are included in the corresponding chapter.